Make Your Mark
in the
WORKSPACE

James Espey was born in Livingstone, Zambia, in 1943 and educated in Cape Town, South Africa, before being transferred to London in 1977.

He holds BCom and MBA degrees, as well as two action learning PhDs in Marketing and Strategic Planning.

James spent fifty years in business, starting in the grocery trade before moving into the liquor industry and later becoming a consultant and a non-executive director of a wide variety of companies.

James has spent a large part of his career working internationally, building and creating brands and also identifying and selecting people who have gone on to "make their mark". He was personally responsible for the launch of Malibu, Johnnie Walker Blue Label and Chivas Regal 18, as well as for the building of Baileys in its formative years.

James has written numerous articles and has also given periodic guest lectures at various business schools in the UK and abroad. He is most proud of helping to create The Keepers of the Quaich, Scotland's leading whisky society, which honours those who make a contribution to this great industry.

In June 2013 he was awarded an OBE for Services to the Whisky Industry in the Queen's Birthday Honours List.

ENDORSEMENTS

"I have had the pleasure of knowing James for forty years and have always admired his level of enthusiasm and ability to bring people together and get things done through his strong leadership skills. This book addresses so many issues known to us but often forgotten.

It is so refreshing to have an easy read that deals with the basic principles of good healthy business, as well as tapping into the successful career of James Espey. Thanks for sharing this with us."
—**Trevor Fish, CEO, Interwil Group, South Africa**

"I read James Espey's book from cover to cover in one sitting. It is very readable and full of common sense and decency. It is not just for the young and ambitious; the hardened, aging and cynical will find it a refreshing reminder of how things should be and how they should manage themselves in everyone's best interests."
—**Tim Isaac, Chairman, Ogilvy & Mather, Asia Pacific (2008–2012)**

"Having known James Espey for over twenty-five years, I have seen at first hand his endless enthusiasm and many achievements in business. *Making Your Mark* brings together all his experiences gained in a long and very successful career, which will benefit many in an easy-to-read manner."
—**Anthony Fuller, Chairman, Fuller, Smith & Turner PLC (1982–2007)**

"James, for a number of years, served as President of The Whisky Group. I would attribute his outstanding success in that capacity to his highly motivational leadership skills, communications brilliance and marketing expertise. This book is a must read for those who wish to attain greatness in their business life."
—**Edward McDonnell, President, The Seagram Wine and Spirits Group (1980–1996)**

"I have known James for more than thirty-five years. He is imaginative, flexible, capable and fun. He has inspired me and has remained a close and trusted friend. This offering of his learnings from his own extensive and successful career is relevant for all aspiring business leaders no matter what culture they're from. It is his take on his own wide experience and, because he is an excellent observer and listener, also the opinions and strengths of the executives he's dealt with over a long lifetime. It gives a great set of guidelines, lightly expressed and easily absorbed."

—Sir Douglas Myers, Former CEO and Chairman,
The Lion Nathan Brewing Group,
New Zealand (1988–1998)

"I have had the good fortune to have known and indeed worked with James over many years. He is truly a lateral thinker and an extraordinarily able communicator. These largely verbal skills are often hard to transmit in writing. This book shows that James fully succeeds in both. A great and instructive read."

—Sir George Bull, Joint Group Chairman,
Diageo PLC (1997–1998)

"The most important brand that everyone must learn to manage is themselves. James Espey was both stylish and successful in his career, and this guide offers shrewd marketing advice to executives at all stages of their business life cycle."

—Hugh Burkitt, Former Chief Executive,
The Marketing Society

"James is an inspirational figure – he is uniquely gifted with his ability to convey complex messages via simple motivational, and, where appropriate, emotive language. I have worked for and with James over the past thirty years – this book captures how he thinks, works and operates . . . his passion for life and work is very infectious."

—Mike Keiller, Former CEO,
Morrison Bowmore Distillers Ltd

"In 1999 James became a Non-Executive Director of A.G. BARR PLC, a long-established family business which, during his twelve years on the Board, grew to become a FTSE 250 company. His outgoing

personality, clarity of thought and passion for the marketing of both the company's business and its soft drinks brands made a significant contribution to our success over both that time and beyond."
— **Robin Barr, former Chairman, A.G. BARR**

"A light entertaining read with some gems of wisdom."
— **Paul Ealsh, CEO, Diageo PLC (2000–2013)**

"James Espey's powerful book will help you achieve career success, "build your brand" and find your own true north going forward. As an Executive Coach, I make it a "must read" for all my clients – and to great effect; executives find it an A-Z journey in their process of personal branding and making it to the top. An easy read with compelling tips and advice culled from years of experience in business - I cannot recommend this book highly enough!"
— **Derek Wilson MBE,**
Chevalier de L'Ordre National du Mérite

Make Your Mark
in the
WORKSPACE
How to Build Your Personal Brand

JAMES ESPEY OBE

RUPA

Published by
Rupa Publications India Pvt. Ltd 2023
7/16, Ansari Road, Daryaganj
New Delhi 110002

Sales centres:
Bengaluru Chennai
Hyderabad Jaipur Kathmandu
Kolkata Mumbai Prayagraj

Copyright © James Espey OBE, 2020, 2023

Original English language edition published by Cherish Editions Suite 4
The Foundation Centre Navigation House 48 Mill Gate, Newark Nottinghamshire,
NG244TS, United Kingdom, Arranged via Licensor's Agent: DropCap Inc.

All rights reserved.
No part of this publication may be reproduced, transmitted,
or stored in a retrieval system, in any form or by any means,
electronic, mechanical, photocopying, recording or otherwise,
without the prior permission of the publisher.

The views and opinions expressed in this book are
the author's own and the facts are as reported by him
which have been verified to the extent possible,
and the publishers are not in any way liable for the same.

P-ISBN: 978-93-5702-129-6
E-ISBN: 978-93-5702-130-2

First impression 2023

10 9 8 7 6 5 4 3 2 1

The moral right of the author has been asserted.

Printed in India

This book is sold subject to the condition that it shall not,
by way of trade or otherwise, be lent, resold, hired out, or otherwise
circulated, without the publisher's prior consent, in any form of binding or
cover other than that in which it is published.

*To my wife and daughters, who have inspired
and supported me through all the years.*

CONTENTS

Foreword ... xv
How to get the most out of this book ... 1

Planning your career ... 3
  1: Who do you want to be? ... 3
  2: SWOT analysis ... 5
  3: Who should you seek to work for? ... 7
  4: The ideal job ... 8
  5: Writing a curriculum vitae (CV) ... 9
  6: Communication soft skills and you ... 12
  7: Environmental analysis: a prerequisite to good forward thinking ... 14

You've got the job! ... 17
  8: The importance of a good contract ... 17
  9: Willing horses get overloaded ... 18
  10: Objectives and appraisals ... 19
  11: Friends in the office – true or false? ... 21
  12: Company politics ... 21
  13: Tips on handling a new boss ... 23
  14: You and promotion ... 24
  15: How long should you stay? ... 26

Good personal style and attributes ... 27
  16: Courtesy and treating people properly ... 27
  17: Nothing beats face-to-face interaction ... 29
  18: The harder you practise, the luckier you get ... 30

19: Everyone can make a good speech	31
20: Punctuality: not just a virtue, but a necessity	33
21: How to prioritise tasks and manage your concerns	35
22: Ambition is healthy, but do not believe in your own hype	37
23: Fiscal Integrity	38
24: Personal health and wellbeing	39
25: Admitting you are wrong	40
26: Never live on your bonus	41
27: The use and abuse of technology	42
28: Who is your boss?	46
29: Family and friends	47
30: A summary of professionalism	47
Basic financial logic	**51**
31: Turnover – profit and cash	51
32: Some useful ways to manage cash flow	52
33: Working with suppliers	54
Retailing	**55**
34: Fundamental principles of retailing	55
35: Retail is detail	57
Simple marketing logic	**59**
36: What is marketing?	59
37: Intrinsic and extrinsic variables	61
38: Marketing myopia	63
39: Maslow's need hierarchy	64
40: The life cycle of a brand manager	66
41: The consumer does not have a financial year	67
42: Effective selling	68
43: Everyone is involved in marketing	69
44: The key to good marketing communication	71

The role of advertising in a nutshell   **71**
  45: Get out of your ivory tower and meet the real customers   73
  46: The 80:20 rule for good businesses   75
  47: Creativity, innovation and new brand development   76
  48: Product life cycle and growing too fast   80

Corporate culture   **83**
  49: What sort of corporate culture is there?   83
  50: Don't confuse the person with the position   85

Family companies   **87**
  51: The essence of a good family company   88
  52: Family shareholders   89
  53: Succession   90

Doing business internationally   **93**
  54: Multicultural adaptability   94
  55: Appreciating different cultures   95
  56: Business travel advice   98
  57: Go and grow where the action is   103

Building your brand   **107**
  58: Brands have life cycles   107
  59: Creative obsolescence: the key to future success   110
  60: "You" the brand   111
  61: Do you know who you really are?   113

Leadership   **115**
  62: What good leaders do   115
  63: People work with you, not for you   118
  64: Do not be a micro-manager   119
  65: Bad news, risk-taking and failure   121

66: Optimism v. pessimism and balance	122
67: Communication is a two-way street	123
68: Politics and decision-making	123
69: Effective meetings	124
70: The Grandfather System and an open-door policy	126
71: Being the new boss: the first 100 days	127
72: All staff will watch you for leadership signals	129
73: Parting with people	133
74: Joining the board	134
75: Top Dog – the boss of a PLC	135

Other things to consider — **137**

76: What really matters?	137
77: The use and abuse of consultants	139
78: Mergers and acquisitions	141
79: Clarifying leadership and communication	143
80: The good and bad of economic fluctuations	145

Changing jobs — **149**

81: Be a good leaver	150
82: The grass isn't always greener on the other side of the fence	151
83: Getting fired is not always bad!	152

Starting your own business — **157**

84: Why are you starting a business?	157
85: Finding the perfect partner	158
87: The hockey-stick rule	160
88: Managing growth	161

Building a non-executive career — **165**

89: Where to start	165
90: Key role of a non-executive director	166
91: Audit committees	167

92: Remuneration committees	169
93: Private companies and financial responsibilities	170

Winding down	**171**
94: Making the break	171
95: It has to end sometime	173
96: Talent-spotting	173
97: There is no such thing as retirement, just a new direction	174
98: Self-employment v. corporate life	175
99: You never stop learning	177
100: Anno Domini: Father Time and the art of the possible	177

Conclusion	179
Acknowledgements	181

FOREWORD

What drove my entrepreneurial spirit?

I was born in Livingstone, Zambia, in 1943, back when it was known as Northern Rhodesia.

My paternal grandfather was an Irishman who had emigrated to South Africa, and who joined the South African Infantry in 1915 and fought in France. He survived Delville Wood and Passchendaele, but was killed by a sniper in 1918, leaving my father and his brother to be raised by their widowed mother in Cape Town. My grandfather's death shaped my father's upbringing, and consequently my own, which made my visit to his grave on the centenary of his death quite poignant and emotional.

My maternal grandfather was an Australian who had fought in the Boer War and ended up staying in Northern Rhodesia. Unfortunately, he died before my mother was born, and my granny not too long after that. My mother was brought up by her grandfather, my great-grandfather Powell.

Great-Grandfather Powell was Postmaster of the Rondebosch Post Office, and got to know Cecil Rhodes, the Prime Minister of the Cape Colony. When Rhodes died, Powell was a pallbearer at his funeral and carried the wreath sent by Queen Alexandra, which was a great honour!

Rhodes commissioned my great-grandfather to open up the telegraphy from Cape Town to Bulawayo in Southern Rhodesia (now Zimbabwe). The family made the trip there first by train, then coach and horses, and finally by ox wagon. Once there,

Powell became the first Rhodesian postmaster. He later became the secretary of The Cleveland Bridge Company, and was involved in building the Victoria Falls Bridge. They initially lived in huts by the side of the Zambezi, with curious hyenas for neighbours, but they persevered, and in 1904, they owned the first house in Livingstone with a tin roof.

So, as you can see, hard work and perseverance is in my blood!

My father had to leave school early for financial reasons, and he became a police officer in Northern Rhodesia. When he was thirty-one, he clip-clopped into town on his horse, met my mother – then nineteen – and married her in 1942. I was born the next year, and my brother followed soon after.

Like my parents before me, I had an emotionally deprived childhood. My parents divorced in 1949, when I was six and my brother five, and that was the last time I ever lived at home.

My brother and I were sent to boarding school 2,500 miles away in Cape Town – a trip that took four days and four nights by rail. By the end of our schooling, we'd spent some six months on a train.

My father remarried in 1952, and I only saw him twice a year – and often in a different town, too, since his job moved him around a lot. I also saw my mother twice a year until I was seventeen, when she emigrated to Australia. Even now, my excuse at home is that I'm absolutely useless at plugs and cooking, but the truth is that I'd never had a normal home upbringing where I learnt to do those things.

Boarding school was tough. The teachers were strict, and my brother and I were two of the poorer students there. I had to learn to be totally emotionally reserved, and to keep everything to myself – it was a sign of weakness to show emotion. There was no understanding of mental health when I was young.

Fortunately, we were quite good at sport and reasonably intelligent, and that made a big difference.

What's my experience in business?

I was fortunate enough to go to Cape Town University to do a BCom degree. After two years I switched to being a part-time student as I was tired of having no money, and for the next three years, I studied part-time while working at the Cape Town Chamber of Commerce and waiting tables two nights a week. I also kept up my passion for sport. I was on a salary of 100 South African Rand a month (about £6 in today's money) – just about enough to live on. It was tough, but for the first time in my life I was financially independent.

When I graduated, I intended to become a Chartered Accountant, but the pay as an Articled Clerk was appalling and not enough to live on. Luckily, I majored in Marketing as well as Accounting. Accordingly, I joined the grocery trade as the Assistant Marketing Manager of Spar South Africa. My job was to ease the transition into self-service retail (at that time, there was only counter service and the shopkeepers would get your shopping for you), and I learnt a lot from it.

I was very thin with bad acne and no money, and I was very self-conscious, but I got by. I had a battered old Volkswagen, shared a house with friends, and life was getting better. In 1966, I helped launch the new-fangled MBA degree at a lunch, which I organised for the Cape Town Chamber of Commerce, and decided to study for the degree in 1968.

My MBA was transformational, both for my finances and for my career. Once I had my degree, I joined Coca-Cola South Africa. My practical thesis was a study to determine the feasibility of marketing canned, carbonated drinks in South Africa – at that point in time, soft drinks were only sold in rented glass bottles, which you had to return to the store to get your deposit back. My theory was that, in Apartheid South Africa, black communities would welcome the opportunity not to have to rely on (often surly) white store owners – and I was right. I got very good work experience at Coca Cola and I was offered the job of Canning

Manager at the end of 1969.

I was, however, headhunted to be the National Sales Manager of Gilbeys South Africa, the South African wine and spirits subsidiary of the British company, International Distillers and Vintners Ltd (IDV).

"If you want something done, ask a busy person."

In 1970, aged twenty-six, I was the youngest member of the sales force and the boss to boot – an interesting challenge. I inherited a sales force of white, middle-aged semi-alcoholics, all with chauffeurs and expense accounts bigger than their salary. I wanted to overturn the imbalance of the hard-drinking culture.

Furthermore, merchandising and self-service was also shaping the future of liquor retail sales.

Obviously I had a few objections to overcome, but I worked hard to change the culture. I introduced the first ever multicultural sales conference, and employed and promoted minority sales executives (men and women alike) and even a teetotaller – a rarity in the alcohol business.

My next step was to work for head office, and in 1977, the famed Chairman of Guinness, Sir Anthony Tennant, transferred me to London to become IDV's Group Marketing Director. Sir Anthony wanted to federalise the group and market our brands effectively across the world.

While British, I was the first non-Englishman ever brought to the UK for IDV. It might sound odd, but it didn't happen in those days. I was often referred to as "a savage from the colonies", and was given a six-month trial. If I passed, I would join the company board; if not, I would be shipped back to South Africa.

So, I gave up the PhD I was working on, and took the global career challenge.

I wanted to make the most of my transfer to London. I played rugby and cricket, so I was very socially active, and I met my now-wife through my work. However, I found the politics of the business world shocking. I was pretty direct (maybe because of my South African background) but I found the lack of honesty and the political bureaucracy frightening in many corporations.

My first job as the newly appointed Group Marketing Director was to be heavily involved in building Baileys Irish Cream, which was invented by my business partner, Tom Jago, and with his support, I personally launched Malibu in 1979. Alongside this, I completed a part-time PhD on the future of IDV Worldwide, entitled "The Development of a Worldwide Strategy for International Distillers & Vintners Limited".

In 1982 I took over running the UK domestic operation and a team of some 4,000 people. The UK profits had been flat for a few years and accordingly, I completed a second PhD entitled "The Process and Formulation of a Strategy for IDV (UK) Limited", to transform and revitalise the domestic company.

As part of my thesis, I got the advice of sixty-seven managers on building a successful strategic vision, which I then used to improve the business. This included giving the staff a greater sense of belonging to the company, and treating them with compassion and respect. The upshot of it all was that profits nearly trebled in four years.

You empower people by encouraging them – that's how companies and brands are made.

Finessing my brand

By this time, I was forty-three with two children to educate. Having come from South Africa, I was not on the British pension scheme, which was a serious concern to me at this stage of my life. So, in 1986, I left IDV to pursue an opportunity at the then-new United Distillers (now Diageo, the world's number one liquor company) as the Deputy Managing Director. I brought Tom Jago onboard and we launched The Classic Malts and Johnnie Walker Blue Label in the late 1980s.

Alongside my work, I helped found The Keepers of the Quaich, the leading Scotch whisky society. It honours those who have made a significant contribution to the whisky industry across the world – a bit like a knighthood for those in the Scotch industry. Through The Keepers I was privileged to meet many significant speakers, including Prince Charles, Princess Anne, and Ronald Reagan, whose speech we wrote for him. He was charming and humble, and he made a big impression.

In 1992, I joined Chivas Bros as Chairman. I was 49 at the time and this was clearly going to be my last corporate job. Having learnt from my experience at IDV, I negotiated two years' notice post an initial three-year contract.

I wanted Chivas Regal to compete with Johnnie Walker Blue Label, so in 1997 I launched Chivas Regal 18 against the wishes of the company chairman (whose father had invented Chivas Regal 12 and said there would never be an 18).

I was fired.

Putting what I've learnt into practise

All my life, I had been a brand man. I had worked hard and had been ambitious, but I tried not to let it go to my head. I had always been driven by my memories of being surrounded by rich students spending Daddy's money – I couldn't stand to be that flashy and careless. Despite having had a successful corporate career, I hate wasting money. I drive a mid-series BMW, and my wife a Golf. If someone gave me a Rolls Royce, I would sell it the next day; it's simply not me.

I always wanted to look after my family; I wanted to make sure that we would never want for anything and that my daughters would have the best education – which, fortunately, they did. But I had always been extremely reserved inwardly when it came to my emotions, even when I matured and things improved. I just didn't know how to let go. I once had a problem with a boss who (frankly) saw me as a threat to his career. Every time the phone rang, I would wonder what it was about – it was never to praise; it was always to find fault, and even though I seemed strong on the outside, I took things seriously and I worried about it emotionally.

So, while I was seen to be a reasonably good achiever, I was paying a high price.

While out of work, my shares (which had been doing fairly well) crashed, and I lost a seven-figure sum of money. I thought I had nothing and that I would have to start again. I had a serious breakdown and finished up in The Priory Hospital.

It was a high price to pay for a lifetime of hard work, but fortunately I never lost my perseverance and nose for business.

When I recovered from my breakdown, I started a new career as a Non-Executive Director on a number of boards, including Church Shoes Limited; Fuller, Smith & Turner PLC (London Pride); and A G Barr PLC (Irn Bru), amongst others.

I also set up my stall to invest in and help small start-ups, knowing of course that not all would succeed. One of these start-ups was Mimecast, an anti-virus software invented by a young South African named Peter Bauer. This company, founded in my home in 2003, is now worth over $3 billion with more than 1,600 employees!

When I was sixty-five, I spotted a gap in the market for rare spirits, so I created my own company with Tom Jago (then eighty-two). We called it "The Last Drop Distillers", with the aim of being "The World's Most Exclusive Spirits Collection". We focused largely on Whisky and Cognac, but we also produced an interesting Tawny Port variation – a twin pack with one bottle from 1970 and a second from 1870. Things were going well.

Sharing my expertise

One of my concerns about society is greed and short-termism, and I was proven right in 2015. My business was badly hurt by a major company that took control of the whisky firm who were doing everything for The Last Drop Distillers. This company got rid of the CEO, (my friend) and dumped me. Suddenly I had nowhere to go. I thought I would have to sell my home, and that my life was going to crash at seventy-two.

Once again, I finished up in The Priory. This time, however, my consultant suggested I have Electro Convulsive Therapy (ECT). It's a procedure carried out under a general anaesthetic, in which a brief electric current applied to either side of the head triggers a small seizure. This causes a reaction in the brain chemistry and "resets" it. According to my psychiatrist, it boosts the levels of neurotransmitters in the brain which are low in depression (much as antidepressants do but in a more dramatic way). I had eight of these sessions, which "rebooted" my brain, resolved my depression, restored my functioning and saved my life.

This happened in 2016, and during this time, my whisky company was sold successfully to a large American group while Mimecast (mentioned earlier) floated on the stock market. This was transformational for me, and the point at which I decided to spend the rest of my life helping others.

Now, I give back to society through various charities, especially ones that promote mental health awareness. I've built two wells in remote Zambian villages, bringing water to over 600 families, and am paying for the education of two children in Livingstone, where I was born. I also fund a scholarship for a disadvantaged student to go to my old school in Cape Town.

I continue to help a number of people with their start-ups and happily provide pro bono advice to young people seeking career guidance.

This is where this book factors in.

"Learnings from the University of Life"

Over my many years in business, I've observed things I did and didn't like, and started writing them down. Now, I want to share them.

I have long thought that books on management aimed at students and upwardly mobile business executives are far too complex, tending to use high-brow academic words that obscure what they are actually suggesting. After fifty years of experience and diligent reading, this conclusion has never waned. Accordingly, I decided to write a simple book – not in terms of content, but in style.

Drawing on my experience in marketing and senior management, I thought I would put into words some simple hard truths – some learnt through observation, others learnt painfully – about what you need to succeed in the world of business.

Let me start by saying that everything revolves around the concept of **brands**. Life is about building a brand; everything is, in effect, a brand. Countries are brands, people are brands and, of course, we purchase brands as we travel around. Think of Great Britain during the war years under Churchill and later – Thatcher, Blair, Brown, Cameron, May, and now Boris Johnson – each one shapes the "UK" brand. Think of the United States under Roosevelt, Eisenhower, Reagan, Clinton, Bush, Obama and now Trump; South Africa during the years of apartheid and then the great Nelson Mandela – wherever you go, countries are shaped by the people who run them. More locally, we are shaped by the lives we live, and we are influenced every day by the brands in front of us.

Most readers of this book will be ambitious, youngish people eager to establish their own brand by "making their mark" as they make their own way through life. I want to help give young executives and entrepreneurs the chance to thrive in their environments. I want to teach them that a good leader accepts their mistakes and learns from them.

I hope these chapters, full of simple yet sound truths, are positive and helpful, and if you, the reader, take only two or three useful tips from them I will be more than satisfied. I want to encourage people to *try*. As I always say, "you never reach the other side if you never leave the shore".

HOW TO GET THE MOST OUT OF THIS BOOK

If you wish to build your personal brand and succeed in business, this book is for you.

This is clearly not a novel, nor is it an academic textbook. Rather, it is a collection of learnings gleaned from the start of a career through to retirement and beyond. If you are just starting out in the commercial world, then I suggest you read from the beginning, clearly focusing on what is relevant to you as you aim to find a job and avoid the inevitable dangers within any organisation.

On the other hand, you may be very comfortable in your present job and therefore not need to learn how to write a CV etc. But what you *should* be interested in are the pitfalls lurking within companies, and how better to grasp the opportunities that will present themselves. In this case, you may go straight to the relevant section.

If you are nearing the end of your career, you may seek advice on how to be an effective non-executive director, or even how to start your own business. Use the Contents list at the start of this book to suit your needs and to guide you to what you deem relevant to your situation.

Finally, this book is not intended to be prescriptive, but to help establish signposts on your journey.

PLANNING YOUR CAREER

A journey of a thousand miles begins with a single step.
Lao Tzu, philosopher

IF YOU DON'T KNOW WHERE YOU'RE GOING, ANY ROAD WILL TAKE YOU THERE.

1: Who do you want to be?

What are you seeking to achieve with your life – starting now?

If you don't know where you are going, any road will take you there. If you don't know where you are, will a map help you?

The point of these simplistic remarks is that, if we are going to make something of our lives, we must have goals – be they short-term or long-term – and identify a roadmap to achieving them.

You may decide that you wish to be the Prime Minister or President, but that is an unrealistic and very long-term goal.

Alternatively, and more realistically, you can decide "I will acquire a job in X area, and make successful decisions that will lead to promotion and, eventually, to being top in my field."

I believe all of us should at least set some goals for the short to medium term. A degree, for example, will enable you to read, analyse, synthesise and write in your field, and will provide a launch pad from which you can decide where to go next. You might choose to focus on politics and economics or marketing because you ultimately want a degree in business. You may decide to do a classics degree (despite being unsure what to do with it) because you never know what might come of it – perhaps a career in law, for example.

My point is, **make a start** and **make a commitment**, both of which will influence your journey through life.

You then need to think about what field of business appeals to you – finance, production, human relations or marketing, for example. There may well be a defining moment early on – usually (if not always) accidental – that sets you off in one direction or another.

It's also good to talk to your family and friends who will, I hope, give you an honest assessment of yourself (possibly guided by what you have achieved in your life so far). This isn't always easy, but it will show courage, humility and integrity.

As John F. Kennedy said in his 1960 North Carolina speech, "Efforts and courage are not enough without purpose and direction."

WHEN YOU JOIN A COMPANY, WHAT DO YOU WISH TO ACHIEVE?

Surely it's not just to collect a pay cheque? If you become a graduate trainee, then clearly that's because the firm has seen something in you that makes them want you on board.

If you are already in a job, you should constantly assess how it is panning out and set yourself reliable, short to medium-term goals. You probably have long-term ambitions to be a general manager or a chief executive – even company chairman – but what steps will you be taking to get there?

I thought first about getting into law or accounting before finally deciding that marketing was where my future lay. Accordingly, my career revolved around marketing and sales en route to general management.

Whichever field you choose, **think at least three years ahead**. How well you do in your present job will influence the future, and you should break the time between then and now into goals, leading from your present role to the next. If you are a brand manager, for example, you should consider wanting to be a group brand manager, then a marketing manager, and eventually a marketing director. At some stage you may wish to switch into general management, so you will want to prepare for that too, when the time comes.

2: SWOT analysis

Clearly, to be in with a chance of promotion, you have to perform to the highest standard. It is, therefore, advisable to seek help to address any areas of weakness.

Let me refer you to an old-fashioned tool, affectionately known as "SWOT", which I believe still has its uses for working out which areas you should work on in terms of self-improvement.

SWOT stands for "Strengths, Weaknesses, Opportunities and Threats", and the idea is to think about what each of these categories means for you.

WHAT ARE YOUR STRENGTHS?
These may include determination, fiscal capability or good organisation, for example. List them all.

WHAT ARE YOUR WEAKNESSES?
Do you feel you are not good at decision-making, for example, or that you are not a very clear thinker or communicator? List these weaknesses as well.

WHAT ARE THE OPPORTUNITIES OPEN TO YOU?
Hopefully, many. List them all.

WHAT ARE THE THREATS TO YOUR ADVANCEMENT?
In some cases, they may simply be financial – you cannot afford to exist on your current income, for example, and you have to decide what sacrifices are worthwhile; or you may not have the money to complete your studies and therefore have to resort to loans. List these threats too.

> I borrowed money to pay for my university studies, but this wasn't sustainable, and after two years I decided to study part-time so that I could undertake a full-time job. I worked 9–5 while attending lectures four nights a week and on Saturday mornings too. Plus, I obviously had to find time to study.
>
> This was hard, of course, but while it took me an extra two years to complete my degree, I was in a better place financially. Not only that, but I also gained useful business experience which helped secure my next job in retail marketing.
>
> Hard work and focus can only be positive, especially in your youth.

Once you have read this chapter, may I suggest you sit down and identify your goals quite clearly, do a SWOT analysis and then reflect on it. Set yourself an immediate goal of completing it and sharing it with people you can rely on, including trusted work colleagues, within the next week.

It may be painful and difficult, but honesty is the best policy. Think of it this way: if you have bad breath or dress sloppily, who is going to tell you?

When I interview people, their appearance and communication skills – both oral and written – have always influenced my opinion of them, so take note of those skills if you wish to be hired. Equally, if you have identified that you are not numerate, you should not expect a job in finance!

3: Who should you seek to work for?

It could be Save the Children or some other charity; it might be a well-known retail group, like Walmart or Tesco; a car manufacturer such as General Motors, BMW or Tesla, or it could be a dynamic IT company such as Google or Facebook etc.

If you are taking a long-term view, carefully consider whether a prospective company is selling today's products or planning tomorrow's future. Would you, for example, join General Motors today? You might, but on the other hand you may decide that they are almost past their sell-by date. After all, they've long had the technology to produce the environmentally friendly cars of tomorrow – so why didn't they? Do you think it was short-term greed – i.e. not really dealing with all the environmental considerations, thus focusing on profit? Was it short-sightedness? Or was it simply top-management arrogance?

At the turn of the century, before the recession hit, working for a bank and the prospect of big bonuses seemed the promised land to many. Now, however, in an increasingly technological world, you may well want to have a close look at dynamic and rapidly changing companies such as Amazon or Apple.

The important thing to look at is where a company is going. See if they have taken the correct steps to adjust their strategy in order to be successful in the future.

RETAILING

Fifty years ago, joining a major retail group was an exciting career opportunity, be it Walmart, Tesco, Marks & Spencer etc. Since the turn of the century, and especially in the last few years, we've seen the high street under extreme pressure, with online retailing and home delivery growing rapidly along with the rise of seriously competitive discount outlets such as Aldi and Lidl. A dynamic, forward-looking company culture should be adaptable and flexible, having closely studied and taken cognizance of the rapidly changing environment around them.

CONCLUSION

When looking at companies, try to study the top management and purported strategy and see if they are taking a dynamic, long-term view.

For example, looking back at the 2008 banking crisis, were the top management long-term strategists or were they driven by ego and short-term profit? Try to determine if your prospective company really cares about the future, or is it all about their own lifestyle and short-term bonuses?

You are building your personal brand and you want to make sure that there is a sound medium- to long-term future within the company you seek to join.

As Confucius says, "Choose a job you love and you will never have to work a day in your life."

4: The ideal job

The ideal job may not be easy to find, but if you get it right, the result will be very rewarding.

In a perfect world, the perfect job is not just about money but about earning respect from your colleagues, looking forward to going to work, and ensuring that your contribution – no matter how small – is improving the business.

I liken it to a balanced four-legged table:

Leg 1: Respect or, better still, admire the people you work with.

Leg 2: Visibly prove your worth to the business.

Leg 3: Make some money.

Leg 4: Have fun.

When one of these legs falls short, your table will be unbalanced and not fit for purpose.

There is no reason why you shouldn't have fun. Working sixteen hours a day relentlessly can hardly be a viable way of life (beyond those days when you're trying to hit a tight deadline, of course). You have been warned!

Why not take a moment to think of your own career along these lines and see if your table is balanced?

5: Writing a curriculum vitae (CV)

Your CV, be it electronic or paper, is a core document that you may tweak depending on who you are sending it to. It is sent alongside a short covering letter, which should be tailored to suit the company in question and which, where relevant, should repeat your CV headline. It should suggest that you have the appropriate skills needed for the company concerned (or even for a specific job) and request an interview. This is essential!

In our frenetic, computerised society, companies are bombarded with CVs. Some come in letter form via the post, but they're mostly sent electronically.

Most end up being filed WPB (Waste Paper Basket) or fall victim to the delete button, and many companies sadly do not have the courtesy even to acknowledge receipt of an application.

Here are some simple guidelines to follow in order to avoid that.

- At the outset, make it clear how you can help the company you are writing to. Your profile should focus on how you can be useful to them or match a specific job on offer. If possible, make your CV different enough to stand out, but not *too* different!
- The HR manager (or whoever reads the CVs) usually has a very short attention span, so be sure to make it short and to the point. No one is interested in long explanations of what you have done. Remember, all they are interested in is what you can do for them.
- List your job successes and accomplishments in reverse chronological order, from the most recent. Use achievement bullet

points and action statements and not vague terms. Always be succinct.

- List your qualifications, your language skills, technical skills, etc., and at the end – briefly – your interests.
- There is no need to include any referees; they can be supplied on request, and in any event, companies have their own ways of checking up on you.
- Be warned: be truthful at all times. If you are found to have "improved" your grades or job titles, it could be seriously damaging to your career.
- If you are making an unsolicited application, start your CV with a good, strong headline that states quite clearly what you are seeking and why you consider yourself a good candidate. This will be the first thing people reading your CV will see. If they like that headline, they will read further; otherwise, they'll simply delete/file WPB.

For example, in the latter stage of my career, I was seeking non-executive appointments after having been involved in international business for many years, and my CV and letter always started with a short headline:

"Experienced International Brand-Orientated Businessman seeks challenging non-executive appointment."

I did not mention my interest in strategy or developing people because I knew that would emerge at interview stage.

Clearly, we are talking about *you*, so tailor the headline to your circumstances. For example, if you are a brand manager looking for a new challenge, your headline could be:

"Experienced brand manager seeks major marketing challenge."

What is essential is that you send your CV alongside a short covering letter that you've tailored to suit that specific company. It should suggest that you have the appropriate skills needed for the company concerned (or even for a specific job) and request an interview.

ONLINE RECRUITMENT

It is important to be consistent and to succinctly find a way to differentiate yourself from others seeking jobs in today's extremely competitive job market.

There are those who believe that a traditional paper CV is outdated, a view compounded by the proliferation of online platforms such as LinkedIn, Facebook and even Twitter. Personally, I think that you should always have a paper CV at the ready as well as an electronic version.

To reiterate, it is fundamental that whatever you say on your CV must be totally accurate. Never forget that potential employers can track you down online!

REJECTIONS

Please accept at the outset that most of the time, you will not even receive a reply, and when you do, more often than not it will be a rejection.

This is hardly ever likely to be personal; it is simply that far more people apply for jobs than there are jobs available.

So, be persistent and keep your spirits up. Make sure that your family and friends critically appraise your CV in terms of content as well as grammar and spelling. Hopefully they will also be there for you to help with responses from companies, both good and bad.

Good luck!

6: Communication soft skills

Besides being equipped with the obvious technical skills, how do you interact and get on with people?

Far too many young people are not making a smooth transition from education to the workplace because there is a serious mismatch between what employers are looking for and the skills that would-be employees have.

Charm, or your ability to interact with others, makes people more receptive to you and your message and thus they will be more willing to be influenced by and think positively about you. This applies to both business and personal relationships.

A major part of your success in life will be determined by your ability to communicate effectively with others. Some people are natural communicators, but if you're not one of them, rest assured that you, too, can learn to be warm, friendly, likeable and charming, simply by observing and utilising a few of the techniques used by successful people around the world.

A key component is to make others feel important. Pay attention to and be fully engaged with the person you are speaking to. Listen attentively and look them in the eyes. Pause before replying, rather than jumping in.

If you wish to disagree, do so courteously rather than dismissing them with a blunt "what rubbish" or similar. Again, this is the time to ask close friends and family how they really see you, and an important aspect of your SWOT analysis.

PERSONAL APPEARANCE

However cool or casual you may think you are in your private life, appearance is crucial if you're job-hunting. Be neat and tidy. Find out and respect the dress code of the company you're applying to. It may well be that you're applying to an agency where everyone is in jeans. If so, while you should make an effort to fit in, ensure that you are at the smart end of casual. Dressing well not only gives you confidence but, more importantly, it gives people confidence in *you*, which is what you want.

Lack of work experience.

If you're worried about a lack of work experience on your CV, I suggest you pursue placements, graduate schemes or internships – the money is secondary at this stage. Do not hesitate to seek temporary work of whatever nature; it all helps prepare you for your career ahead and adds weight to your CV.

Research by High Fliers (2019) found that "Over a third of recruiters warned that in today's competitive job market, it was either "not very likely" or "not at all likely" that a graduate who'd had no previous work experience at all with any employers would be successful during their selection process and be made a job offer, irrespective of their academic achievements or the university they had attended."

HOW TO MAKE A GOOD IMPRESSION AT AN INTERVIEW: A SUMMARY

1. Always be punctual, and call ahead if there is a genuine problem.
2. Maintain good eye contact and give a firm handshake.
3. Look smart. Two of my personal NO-NOs are scruffy shoes and dirty fingernails, both of which suggest the person does not care much.
4. Be respectful and take your lead from the interviewer in terms of formality.
5. Beware of undue humour, especially with strangers.
6. Smile, be gracious, pay attention – and do not hesitate to say thank you for the meeting.
7. Follow up with a letter, or email if appropriate.

Essentially, when communicating with a prospective employer, your job is to accentuate the positive and limit the potential for being prejudged negatively.

> Some twelve years ago, after a series of interviews, the Chief Executive of a public UK company invited me to be his Chairman. There was another very serious contender, but – as I subsequently learnt – the Chief Executive had a thing about clean shoes, and the clincher was the fact that, unlike the rival candidate, my shoes were spotlessly clean.

7: Environmental analysis: a prerequisite to good forward thinking

Not one of us lives in a vacuum, yet it is amazing how many people just drift along as if everything will fall into place of its own accord. If you're reading this book, you most likely have a clear ambition in life and wish to make the most of your talents. As a starting point, it is vital that you fully understand the environment in which you aim to operate.

We do this in our own private lives, consciously or otherwise. For example, if you want to buy a house or a flat there are a multitude of factors to consider. What is the economic situation like? Can you afford it? Are you able to get a mortgage? What is the best area to live in? Is it better to have a small property in a very good area or a larger property in a less good area? What are the market trends etc.?

These are decisions that have a major impact on our lives, and consequently we usually think through them very carefully. That simple principle is exactly what must be applied whether you're job-hunting or in a position to make serious decisions in a company.

UNCONTROLLABLE VARIABLES

In the classic *Basic Marketing: A Managerial Approach*, first published in 1968 (yes, that long ago), E. J. McCarthy suggested that before a businessman can talk about how they would effectively reach the consumer, he or she must understand that there are a number of uncontrollable factors to consider, even though, by definition, they cannot control them.

First and foremost, let us look at the uncontrollable factors in the macro environment.

- What is the economic situation at a given point in time? (For example, early 2020 saw the emergence of the Coronavirus, the consequences of which must be recognised wherever you seek to work.)
- What about global warming and its impact on society?
- Is it easy to raise finance?
- What is the political climate both in our own country and in the countries with whom we wish to do business?
- Depending on the type of business we are in, what is the cultural and social environment? Is it supportive of or a hindrance to the brands we wish to promote?

These are only a few pointers, but what I'm suggesting is that you need to consider such factors as part of a broader background when making decisions on behalf of your company.

SEMI-CONTROLLABLE VARIABLES

What do I mean by semi-controllable? Well, clearly, existing business practices are what they are now, but can they – with time and commitment – be changed?

- The structure of the organisation can be changed.
- The culture can be changed – although it will take time.
- What sort of marketing commitment is there? Will it be consistently available?
- Most importantly, consider leadership – for change invariably emanates from the top.

There are others, of course, but this gives you an idea.

CONTROLLABLE VARIABLES

Finally, we move to the actual controllable variables. Essentially, these are the resources the company has with which to influence the business – marketing, sales, production, IT, finance, personnel, distribution, etc. This is not an exhaustive list but merely some suggestions, and if you are going to succeed in the future, you must also have a good understanding of the external environment and the areas you cannot influence *as well as* the internal environment and the areas you can influence.

This should help you decide what industry to seek work in. Once you've decided that, you'll need to consider which firms within that industry offer the most promise, and within the firm itself, where you think you will be able to maximise your potential.

Nothing is easy, but some sound analysis will hopefully help you more effectively identify the opportunities in the future.

PRET A MANGER

I am a great fan of Pret A Manger, the dynamic fresh, natural fast-food chain.

I recently happened to be eating there, when I noticed an information board. It indicated that the food was handmade in that shop's kitchen, using local, natural ingredients without additives or preservatives. It also stated that, at the end of the day, Pret A Manger gave any unsold food to charity and that they used recyclable packaging.

What does this tell me?

It tells me that they are growing quickly, and that they positively understand their consumer base and the fast-changing environment. They understand today's concern about healthy ingredients and environmental damage while serving fresh food rapidly and with a smile for people in a hurry.

YOU'VE GOT THE JOB!

*If you would hit the mark, you must aim a little above it;
every arrow that flies feels the attraction of earth.*
Henry Wadsworth Longfellow, poet

8: The importance of a good contract

I strongly recommend that – if at all possible – you have a sound contract. That contract is the only security you will have, because if the company decides to do away with your services, you will be at the mercy of the HR people and the rule of law. At the end of the day, you versus the corporation is rather like David versus Goliath.

Very few people have long contracts today, but it is reasonable to demand that the period of notice is quite clear, e.g. three or six months.

If a company is wooing you, you are in a far stronger negotiating position without appearing greedy. If you are being relocated internationally, ensure that your contract covers you for a reasonable period of time, with all relevant expatriate expenses incorporated, including repatriation to your own country at the end of your placement.

Finally, ensure a written contract before you join, and *never* accept a position with a verbal promise. Sadly, the days of a handshake being binding are over.

> In 1992, I joined the Seagram Company as the President of the Chivas and Glenlivet Group. I had been (rather flatteringly) chased by the firm for a number of years, and when I finally took on the job of running the Chivas Group I demanded a three-year contract with at least two years' rolling notice. This was ultimately a sticking point because people were not given contracts for more than a year. But I was forty-nine years old and I had learnt from experience, so stuck to my guns and stated clearly that I would give my all to the company – although from what I had observed, people didn't necessarily last with Seagram.
>
> How prophetic! I got my three-year contract with two years' rolling notice and when I fell out with the Chairman of the company some years later (and therefore fell on my sword and had to take early retirement), my contract made all the difference. I at least had the comfort of knowing I was to be paid for two years, which gave me sufficient time to rebuild my life. I was then able to make the switch to a plural career, rather than working for one company.

9: Willing horses get overloaded

It is often said that 10% of the people do 90% of the real work, so when you join a new company as an ambitious, upwardly mobile junior executive, beware of being too much of a willing horse.

You'll be going the extra mile, of course, and working long hours (hopefully effectively). The problem, however, is that your superiors may well offload lots of projects onto you as a result. This can be counter-productive, especially if you report to more than one person. Consequently, you will do five jobs moderately well rather than two or three extremely well, and thus won't receive the recognition you deserve. Instead, you'll be criticised for the quality of your work.

It's quite a conundrum, but one that should be faced early. You need to make it quite clear that you cannot do the work properly unless you are given reasonable time and support. If you fail here, I predict that your annual or bi-annual review will be moderate at best and you will feel unappreciated and demotivated. Work with your line manager to agree manageable targets.

Lastly, it's understandable that you will also wish to enjoy a good social life, but you cannot go out every night and expect to be fresh and ready in the morning. Choices have to be made, and you'll have to learn to say no to going out if you want to succeed and get the work/life balance right. I know – I've been there!

Far too many people have a nine-to-five mentality. Getting the balance right early on – despite your enthusiasm – will be the key to your upward progress.

10: Objectives and appraisals

Ensure that these are agreed and reviewed, ideally twice a year. This is a great opportunity for you to stress your loyalty to the company (no matter what you really think) and to seek guidance from your manager as to how you can advance your career.

OBJECTIVES
Most people are measured against reasonable performance criteria, so expect to have objectives given to you in writing when you join a company. If not, ask for them; it's good to have an understanding from above as to what you are required to do. Most of us already know what our key measurable tasks will be, so there will always

be something unexpected – but this is life. There may also be the odd soft objective, such as "prove that you are a team player". The answer here is a judgement about how well you are collaborating with and getting on with your colleagues.

APPRAISALS

If you are working for a corporation, you should at least have an annual (if not bi-annual) performance review. Most companies do this as a matter of course. If not, ask your boss for an assessment of your performance, and use the review as an opportunity to discuss your own ambitions.

PITFALLS

Sometimes, however, you will have a superior who has a mechanical approach to everything which can create problems for you, especially if you are a lateral-thinking creative individual.

I once had a boss who did everything with metrics. He was a box-ticker who was uncomfortable with unconventional thinking, and the annual appraisal simply meant going through a checklist. On one occasion, I changed my priorities to deal with a major crisis, and consequently saved the company a great deal of money. That didn't matter to him though; he was more concerned that I hadn't fulfilled objective X as well as I should have, despite that being because I diverted my time to successfully solve the bigger problem.

He was patently wrong. While you have to have structure and objectives for appraisals, they are not an end in themselves but more a means to an end – namely the success of the company – as well as guidance for your career.

ALWAYS LET THEM BELIEVE THAT YOU ARE LOYAL TO THE CORPORATION

This is important, so stress that loyalty whatever you think of the business. Let them know that you're eager to develop your career upwards, and find out what training is available to you. For example, find out if they will sponsor you in further education, such as an

MBA or a specialist master's degree. If there are opportunities to be sent abroad, tell them if that interests you. Most importantly, look ahead within a reasonable timeframe and set yourself some goals to help you climb the ladder of success.

11: Friends in the office – true or false?

Some of my greatest friends are people I have met through work, but I only truly found out who they were after I left that particular company. It is important (and also more enjoyable) to have "work friends", but don't build your life around this. Your true friends are the people outside work, and only the passage of time will determine whether those special colleagues become counted amongst them.

All too often, I see supposedly close relationships end as soon as one person loses their job or goes elsewhere. When I lost my job twenty-two years ago, I was both fascinated and saddened to see who called and who didn't. There were some wonderful surprises from people I didn't know well, but there were others who never took the trouble to pick up the phone. One senior colleague, who I wrongly thought was a friend, did not contact me for some nine months until he, too, left the company. Then my phone rang and he suggested that we should get together. I politely declined – I knew he was only getting in touch because he thought I might be useful to him.

It is essential to have a life outside the office that revolves around your family and non-business friends. With time, some of your office colleagues will become good friends, but do be wary and never take genuine office friendships for granted.

12: Company politics

BE POLITICALLY SENSITIVE, NOT POLITICAL
All companies are political animals, and some are more political than others. There are those where there is an open culture, where

people are allowed to say what they think, and there are others where people don't want you to tell them anything and you have to be very careful what you say.

If the culture is good, you get loyalty. If the culture is "revolving door", then loyalty goes out of the door too. The signals invariably come from the attitude and style of top management.

Be wary of any so-called "confidential discussions" with executives you don't know well. It is amazing how things pass around any organisation and, worse, get twisted and woven into a story that wasn't the one that you started. There are negative spin doctors everywhere, and not just in political parties!

So, yes, there are politics and you have to play the game very carefully, but the message is: be politically sensitive at all times. Be aware of what is going on around you, but don't play corporate politics, don't talk about people behind their backs, and don't say things that you will regret.

Never forget what is too readily forgotten – that the ultimate arbiter of success is the consumer and that 80% of our time should be focused externally on them, with only 20% on internal processes.

In my last full-time job, I found that 80% of the time was all too often spent on internal politics and sectional interests, rather than on building brands for the long term. And, as it happens, the company no longer exists. Their brands, however, are prospering, having been acquired by other, better-run companies!

OFFICE GOSSIP AND RUMOURS

It is human nature to indulge in friendly chat, and we all like to talk about people, be they friend or foe. However, while we like to talk and make new friends and sometimes pass on snippets of information, doing so can be dangerous to your career.

Negative gossip travels at the speed of sound, and it is invariably embellished and enhanced, so you must be very careful what you say in the workplace.

It's vital that you grasp this because, if you vocalise negative thoughts about anyone, rest assured that those thoughts will soon be heard all around the office. Senior managers have to be very discreet, so if you're aiming to become one, you should learn to be careful – you don't want a reputation as a gossip. You have been warned!

> Recently, a young friend (we'll call him "Ben") working his way up the management ladder of a retail group was offered a promotion, with the proviso that he did not tell anyone until the following day, when an official announcement would be made. That day, he received a text from a supposedly good friend who had applied for the same position at another branch saying he hadn't been promoted. He asked about Ben, who replied that he had got the job.
>
> The text went viral within the company.
>
> Everyone knew, from the bottom to top management. Ben was called into his manager's office and severely reprimanded. He was told that under the circumstances his promotion was under threat and that a decision would be made the following day. He spent the night raging at himself for his foolishness. The next day he was told that he still had the job, but that he couldn't expect the raise he had hoped for. Ben subsequently hand-wrote a note expressing his thanks to the management for keeping faith in him and assuring them a similar indiscretion would never happen again. It was a useful lesson learnt the hard way.

13: Tips on handling a new boss

It is understandable to be a bit nervous whenever a new boss is appointed, especially if they come from outside the company – and all the more so if the boss brings in colleagues from their previous firm. But remember, while you're assessing the new boss carefully, they will be doing the same to you.

My simple rule is to have a positive attitude to the change. Look enthusiastic and act professionally at all times. More than ever, be wary of gossip and do not indulge in any negative thoughts/actions. If you get the opportunity to meet the new boss, be supportive, welcoming and offer to help in any way you can without being over-flattering. Most importantly, do your job well.

It may be helpful to do some background checks on where the new boss came from and how they are perceived, especially in terms of management style. Remember to take it with a pinch of salt though, because unhappy people in the previous organisation will certainly not paint a good picture.

The first six months are always going to be difficult, so don't get reckless or angry because you're expected to do things differently. You must be adaptable and positive and see how things work out – which will hopefully be for the better.

You must also be wary of criticising the predecessor. Be very careful in what you say. The new boss will be judging whether you are being objective or simply trying to curry favour, which could well backfire.

Ideally, the new boss should be a team player and encourage all to contribute to the future success of the organisation, but this is not always the case.

I once had a new boss who told me, 'When I want your opinion, I will give it to you' – or words to that effect. Such an exchange is an obvious signal that it is perhaps time to move on – but again, be measured and calm in your response, and certainly never leave guaranteed employment without having a new job firmly and contractually in place.

With luck, however, the new boss will be a motivator and a leader who will help and enhance your career.

14: You and promotion

Soon, you should leave the pack and start the corporate climb, which means being responsible for and leading others. But great soccer players do not automatically become great captains, and many who wish to stay in the game later in life do not succeed in management.

You must lead by example, of course, but being a leader is very different to being one of the team.

THE HIGHER YOU CLIMB THE LONELIER IT GETS

While your basic character should not change, there are times when you cannot afford to be one of the team, and will have to stand apart. This isn't arrogance; it's simply accepting that you have a responsibility to exercise leadership.

POLISH YOUR COMMUNICATION SKILLS

Good leaders present ideas clearly, convincingly and accurately, be it written or oral. Good communication is a crucial skill that strengthens and grows teams. You should also ensure you are a good listener – something at which many fail.

START THINKING STRATEGICALLY

An important responsibility of yours will be to harness the thinking of many people and ensure that good ideas surface for the benefit of the organisation. You must think and plan ahead, rather than focusing purely on day-to-day activities.

LEARN TO UNDERSTAND COMPLEXITY AND UNCERTAINTY

Organisations are multifaceted social and political environments. And, as stated earlier (see Environmental Analysis), you have to understand the complexity and uncertainty all around you, and keep yourself informed of all the various issues affecting your business.

MANAGING YOURSELF

Last but not least, in order to manage others successfully, you need to ensure you effectively manage yourself, and that you develop a consistent decision-making and management style understood by everyone in the organisation.

As Jenny Carter (of the University of Cape Town Graduate School of Business) memorably put it, "Leadership is cultivated, not wished into form."

15: How long should you stay?

In bygone times, people joined companies for life. They often worked for one organisation to the end of their careers, got their pension (usually as a percentage of final salary), and looked back with pride on a life spent working for the same company.

In today's world, things have changed dramatically – I honestly think it is now hard to look beyond five years at the same place. But the good news is that there's nothing wrong with changing jobs periodically (within reason), and in your early career it may well be the right thing to do – particularly if signs within the company point to the fact that it might be better to jump ship, rather than waiting around to be pushed.

BE LOYAL, BUT DON'T EXPECT LOYALTY IN RETURN

Moving on may not always be your choice. You may show loyalty in everything you do, but do not expect it in return. Regrettably, few companies are truly loyal to their employees. They may give that impression, but in truth most, if not all of us, are dispensable and your company will have no problem in terminating your services if it decides to save a few pennies. Sadly, most of us are soon forgotten. That is why I always say your true friends are outside the office.

Fortunately, now there is no stigma to being made redundant or even fired. But however you move on, do so with good grace.

GOOD PERSONAL STYLE AND ATTRIBUTES

If it is to be, it's up to me.
Ben Hogan, one of the greatest golfers of all time

BE NICE TO PEOPLE ON THE WAY UP, WITH LUCK, THEY MAY REMEMBER YOU ON THE WAY DOWN.

16: Courtesy and treating people properly

Every single person wants to wake up in the morning looking forward to going to work, and a large part of that is the way we treat people. It costs nothing to say "thank you", be gracious and smile, so why not get into the habit? It sets the tone for your team, makes life more enjoyable and motivates everyone – and everyone benefits.

Courtesy costs nothing and is a reward in itself. I am always appalled when I see arrogant, rude behaviour from senior executives in companies who treat their underlings as commodities rather than as valuable assets. Companies and brands are built on reputation, which can be damaged very easily by such behaviour.

If you work for somebody who shouts at you in front of others, you must examine whether you really want to be in that company.

TREAT EVERYONE WITH RESPECT

A company is as strong as its weakest link and there are many different people in the chain. This includes the staff who answer the phones and look after the mail, cleaning staff, contractors etc. Everyone has a role to play and everyone wants to feel part of an organisation.

You learn from everybody around you. I have often chatted to the security guards at work and picked up fascinating bits of gossip and information that have helped me to make better decisions. When I had the use of a chauffeur, unless I was with a customer or colleague, I always sat in the front. I made a friend of that person, my chauffeur felt part of the company – and again, I learnt a great deal.

So, as you climb the corporate ladder, remember to be nice to everybody. It motivates people and makes them feel proud to be part of your company.

Being nice to people will also reap its own reward: if you treat people decently on the way up the ladder, with a bit of luck they may remember you – or, better still, treat you well – on the way down. As a senior citizen, I find it interesting to witness this from first-hand experience.

Good manners will always win in the long run. In recent years I procured two interesting and rewarding consulting contracts on the recommendation of two successful senior executives who had, some years back, reported to me as juniors in the companies we then worked for. What a delightful payback for courtesy and respect.

> The negative consequences of rudeness are, for me, splendidly exemplified by this incident.
>
> Some years ago, I was checking into a major international airline at Heathrow to fly to New York, and there was an extremely rude man in front of me who was very abusive to the woman at the check-in counter. He was giving her a very hard time in a most arrogant manner about the fact that his flight was delayed – something that was obviously not her fault. What's more, he didn't ask but rather *demand* that he be upgraded, as he had a Gold Card.
>
> Throughout this verbal harangue, the airline employee was charming and gracious. She smiled and treated him with courtesy.
>
> When he moved on and I reached the counter, I complimented her on her graciousness and for being a credit to her employer. I then said, 'And how did you manage to keep your composure when that man was so rude to you?' She said, 'Sir, I had no problem at all. He is flying to New York, but his luggage is going to Karachi.'

17: Nothing beats face-to-face interaction

One of my concerns about modern management and instant electronic communication via email and mobiles is that there is not enough MBWA – Management By Walkabout.

Don't hide in your office. Make a point of talking to people around you. Walk the floor. Visit staff all over the building.

Digital communication is great, but it can also be a cop-out. In one of the companies I worked for, I would get emails from my Finance Director in the next office about the most mundane matters. I walked into his office one day and said, 'Please don't send me an email about a simple question. Why not just come and see me in my office?'

Far too many people hide behind emails nowadays, and it's (sadly) too often a substitute for verbal or visual interaction. Nothing beats eyeball-to-eyeball discussion or, failing that, a conversation over the telephone. Use emails to confirm decisions, not to negotiate; and remember, emails are also open to misinterpretation because people can read and understand them literally (and they're often not very well-written). I repeat: nothing beats face-to-face dialogue. Remember, a handshake is worth a thousand emails!

SHORT NOTES, NOT EVERY WORD

Once, when negotiating with the Chief Executive of a major company in New Zealand, I was accompanied by a young consultant – a bright, earnest recent MBA graduate. After the pleasantries, we got down to business and my young colleague started writing notes furiously. I asked the gentleman across the desk if I could adjourn to speak to my colleague for a minute. When we got outside, I told him never to do that again. We were in a very important face-to-face discussion; it is rude and disrespectful to be acting like a stenographer.

By all means, have a little notepad in which to jot down the odd comment; then, when you get out of the meeting, feel free to write what you like from memory using your notes as your reminder. But switch off your phone and don't sit there busily recording every word, or feel you have to just because you are a junior officer in a meeting.

I accept that people write notes with iPads and similar devices, but please be careful; your job is to establish trust, good chemistry and two-way communication.

18: The harder you practise, the luckier you get

The great South African golfer Gary Player used to say that the harder you practise, the luckier you get. Of course, it's not as simple as that. In the first place you have to have the requisite talent, but the difference between good and great is often about the dedication, the commitment and the application.

In *Outliers: The Story of Success*, Malcolm Gladwell describes the difference between "good" and "great" as 10,000 hours of dedication, practice and perfecting your skills (2008).

Tiger Woods arguably spent more than 10,000 hours perfecting his golf swing from a very early age. Bill Gates, while fortunate enough to be around at the emergence of home computing, no doubt spent at least 10,000 hours developing his computing skills. Soccer players, great athletes, and businessmen with great ideas all make a serious commitment in time and effort. They do not succeed through talent alone.

The message is this: being bright or talented doesn't guarantee success. How you harness that talent, how hard you work at it and, last but not least, how well you work with people will be the key to your success in business.

Good managers will improve their luck in a number of ways, such as establishing networks to keep informed of threats and opportunities, visiting customers and suppliers regularly, carefully reading the relevant trade press and generally keeping up to date with what is happening. Lastly, by being good at envisaging future scenarios, they are forward-thinking. Essentially, a "lucky" manager understands imagination, opportunity and action, and thus the ability to make decisions.

So in order to progress, you need to influence your luck, make sacrifices and prioritise. That doesn't mean you won't be able to enjoy yourself, but if you are going to climb the corporate ladder, you'll have to make certain choices.

How much of a commitment are you prepared to make as an investment in your future career?

19: Everyone can make a good speech

Not everyone is a natural orator but, no matter how nervous you may be, it is always possible to deliver a good speech – providing you prepare properly.

At the beginning of your career, you may feel in awe of the assembled company, especially when speaking to an older audience. Some nervousness is understandable, of course, but if you "think audience", if you remember that they are there to listen to you, and you deliver your presentation carefully, it can be a wonderful opportunity to put across a strong message and command attention – which can't be a bad thing in terms of your career!

Here are some tips to aid you in the process:

1. **Know your subject well and put in the required planning.** Be quite clear about what you wish to achieve, and have a structured, concisely written script.
2. **Slides, if used, should be simple and attention-grabbing** – they are there to assist you in speaking to your audience with authority. Most people use slides to deliver a visual message, but what really counts is you and how you project yourself to your audience.
3. **Never read your speech, but rather refer to bullet points with notes.** After all, you should know your subject and should be able to talk about it without props. Do not rely on technology: it is easy to tell when someone's head is moving from side to side as they read from an autocue.
4. Everyone has their own unique style of speaking, but what is important is to **eliminate bad habits** (your close friends will certainly tell you what they are). Practise your delivery until you are satisfied.
5. When making a speech in a country where English is not the first language, **a few words in the host language never fail to impress.**
6. **Look at your audience**, look the part, vary your tempo and pause for effect – and ensure that you are passionate about the subject without being over the top.
7. No matter whether you feel comfortable with the audience or not, **never show aggression or be defensive**. If you are ever heckled, be graceful in any response.
8. **Do not overrun your allotted time**, and make sure that you allow for pauses, laughs etc as part of your preparation. If you think it is fifteen minutes, know that it is more likely to be twenty.

9. **Always work out how you're going to end your speech** (which should be with a well-prepared final message). Remember to thank your audience for listening to you; your concluding comments are often what the audience will remember most!
10. Finally, **less said effectively is far better than more said hurriedly**.

> Some thirty years ago, I gave a keynote speech at a global conference in Scotland. For the first time ever, I was asked to use an autocue. I was reluctant to embrace this technology and made a point of preparing thoroughly and feeling very comfortable with the subject on the agenda. Halfway through my speech, the lights fused and the hall was suddenly in total darkness. I carried on speaking without my notes for some fifteen minutes and then, when the lights came on, I received an ovation. This is not intended to be an ego trip, but a practical illustration to stress that preparing properly and treating the audience with respect is a fundamental requirement.

20: Punctuality: not just a virtue, but a necessity

I have a simple philosophy which is, if you are not early for a meeting, you are late.

It may sound silly and trite – but think about it: if your plane leaves at 4.40 pm and you arrive at 4.41 pm, you will miss the flight. Likewise, I am always punctual for the theatre, but have noticed recently that, in some theatres, if you arrive after the performance has started, they (quite rightly) won't let you in.

In any event, why not arrive early and enjoy a cup of tea or coffee and relax or, if need be, work while you wait? You will be more relaxed, refreshed and thus in a better frame of mind.

So why, then, are so many people always late for business meetings? It is rude and it creates a bad impression.

Always set yourself a goal of arriving fifteen minutes early for every meeting you wish to attend. Things can easily go wrong in life, as we all know.

By the same token, if visitors have made an appointment to see you, do not keep them waiting for long; it is discourteous, a waste of their time and genuinely bad form. If you are running late, have the courtesy to personally apologise and advise them you will be as quick as possible, or at the very least have someone do it for you. And of course, offer them tea or coffee while they are waiting in reception.

It is a simple tip, but if you follow this mantra and set a good example, you will gain respect and be a much better leader for it.

But if you *are* going to be late…

Sometimes delays or postponements are inevitable; you may be stuck in traffic, for example, or your plane is stacking or – worse still – cancelled. What is important is to deal with it promptly and courteously.

Firstly, always call, even if you are only going to be fifteen minutes late – and apologise in advance.

Secondly, if you miss your flight for one reason or another, then at least offer a solution – "Instead of lunch, could we have dinner or can we meet tomorrow?" for example. Or, if all else fails, perhaps you could have a video conversation if you have a laptop with you.

BUSINESS ATTIRE

First impressions are vital, and it says a great deal if you look neat and tidy when you show up for a meeting or for a client visit. I believe that your appearance also says a great deal about the company you work for. You may like jeans and sneakers, but that is not the norm in business. Even if you have dress-down Fridays, "casual" should be "smart casual".

21: How to prioritise tasks and manage your concerns

In our 24/7/365 digital world, no one seems to have enough time. Perhaps what we all need is a checklist to make sure we manage ourselves properly.

PREPARE A DAILY TO-DO LIST

On one sheet of paper, list what you need to do for the day and prioritise each item. Work through the list from the beginning, starting with the most important task first. At the end of the day prepare the next day's list.

DO THE JOBS YOU DON'T LIKE FIRST THING IN THE MORNING

It is inevitable that there will be a number of jobs that you do not like to do. Usually these are phone calls or jobs that involve dealing with other people. You may need to discuss somebody's unsatisfactory performance with them, call a customer who is particularly unpleasant, or write an email that you've been putting off.

Whatever it is, I earnestly recommend that you do it first thing in the morning because, if you leave it till after lunch, it will simply be postponed again and again. We are all human and I am sure you will recognise this trait.

MAKE THE BEST USE OF YOUR TIME

It is a great time-saving technique if you can develop priorities and (tactfully) decline time-wasting activities. Avoid unnecessary attendance at meetings and, if you are in charge, keep meetings short.

And learn to say no!

KEY WORRIES (THE THINGS THAT KEEP YOU UP AT NIGHT)

It's amazing how often you wake at 4 am worrying about something or other – but you could actually see that as a way of prioritising what's important. Keep a little notebook next to your bed and write down anything you remember at that time. Jotting your thoughts down will usually help you get back to sleep and then you can focus on them in the morning.

These concerns come with the territory of responsibility and management. Accept them and deal with them.

KEEP YOUR DESK TIDY

It's true that the fewer the distractions and the less clutter on your desk the easier it is to focus. The same applies to the burgeoning inbox on your computer.

USE THE WASTEPAPER BASKET MORE OFTEN

When in doubt throw it out! Also, try to take appropriate action on each document or email immediately if possible.

PROTECT YOUR PRIVATE LIFE

We all need time for ourselves and our families. If we ignore this, our health and our personal lives will suffer.

DO NOT HESITATE TO SEEK ADVICE

It is not wrong to seek help. It *is* wrong to blindly go forth in hope.

There is nothing shameful in not being sure about what to do. If you work for a decent company and have a decent boss, he or she would expect you to come and discuss your concerns with them.

I made it clear to those who reported to me that my door was always open when they were stuck with an issue or problem which they were not sure how to solve. However, it is no good going to your boss and saying, "Help! I have a problem; what should I do?" That is simply offloading the issue and shows that you aren't really trying to find a solution.

The correct approach is to say, "I have a problem and a proposal for dealing with it, but I would like your input/help/advice." In this way, your boss is actively involved in sharing both the problem and the solution. And a problem shared is a problem halved. If they're a decent person, you should all be in it together, even if you get it wrong. We all make mistakes and from many of these we learn a great deal.

The earlier you involve your boss the better, even if you think you can fix it. This builds loyalty and ensures that your boss never hears about it from someone else.

It's important to find a constructive way of handling issues to the best of your ability, and one which involves feeling able to draw on the support of the key people around you.

22: Ambition is healthy, but do not believe in your own hype

As you rise up the corporate ladder and become more important because of the position you hold, the invitations arrive, the cars are laid on when you travel, sometimes even private jets are available and, if you are really successful, the paparazzi will be after you.

NEVER CONFUSE THE PERSON WITH THE POSITION

Don't let it go to your head. As the 17th-century dramatist Thomas Otway said, "Ambition is a lust that is never quenched, but grows more inflamed and madder by enjoyment."

It's funny how some successful people think that they have the right to a certain table in a restaurant, an upgrade on an aeroplane or invitations to the hottest arts or sporting events. What they too often forget, however, is that these privileges and invitations are not actually extended to them as people, but to the titles they carry.

> When I was Chief Executive of IDV UK (International Distillers & Vintners, now part of Diageo), I recall being invited by a pompous senior man in the liquor industry to be his guest for a day in a private luxury marquee at the Wimbledon tennis championships. When we got there, in our opening exchange, I said to him with a

smile, 'Thank you for inviting my wife and me, but you know you did not actually invite me here today.'

He said, 'Of course I did; it's a wonderful pleasure to see you and enjoy your company.'

'No,' I replied, 'you did not actually invite me. You invited the Chief Executive of IDV UK Limited.'

'But that's you!' he exclaimed.

'Yes,' I replied. 'But if I lost my job tomorrow, would you still invite me?'

With a smile, he took the point and then we had a wonderful day.

23: Fiscal Integrity

As you build your career, you'll have increasing opportunities to enjoy the benefits of an expense account. There is a simple rule: treat the expense account as if it were your own personal account and never take advantage of the company.

I once worked with an individual who was hard-working and effective in the marketplace but he always took liberties with his expense account and started making false claims, such as taking his wife with him on travels, cheating with restaurant bills and so on. There was a simple result: he was fired.

No matter how good the individual is, if he or she is cooking the books and taking money from the company (which is effectively theft), you cannot ignore it. Having a hand in the till must always be a firing offence. Fiddling expenses is almost as bad.

So while it may be tempting to claim beyond your entitlement, think about it like this: would you be happy to submit your claim on the office noticeboard? I am sure that there are good guidelines to make it clear what is right and what is wrong, but this is what it comes down to: you don't want to damage your career for the sake of a bit of personal greed. It is just a question of simple logic.

GIFTS AND ENTERTAINMENT

This is a more ambiguous area, but simply accept the fact that very rarely do people in business entertain you purely because they like you. Usually, there is a commercial objective, which is to secure business from your company. My advice is to be very careful about what you accept and make sure that it is known openly – otherwise, it may be misconstrued and, at worst, be regarded as bribery.

Some time ago, two colleagues of mine were given Rolex watches as thank-you presents at the conclusion of an international deal. They were uncomfortable and embarrassed, but felt it was inappropriate to reject the gifts. On returning to the UK they declared them to the CEO, who used a Solomon-type judgement to solve the problem. The watches were leased to them at £1 a year for five years. If they left the company in the interim, the watches had to be handed in; otherwise, at the end of the five years they became theirs to keep.

24: Personal health and wellbeing

This may sound obvious, but nevertheless cannot be underestimated: you cannot change your date of birth and the effects of Father Time, but you *can* look after yourself to the best of your ability.

After all, if someone is being interviewed for a job and he or she looks unhealthy and untidy, as though they don't take care of themselves, they are hardly likely to create a good impression.

The old cliché "a healthy body is a healthy mind" is absolutely true. We are all different, but we must still take time to look after ourselves, exercise in a reasonable and balanced way and take care with our appearance.

It is also true that it is easier to exercise in the morning, because at 6 pm the lure of a beer or a glass of wine inevitably wins – especially in winter!

It is all about balance, so try to do something aerobically useful about three times a week and build it into your routine.

STRESS

In the present global downturn I see people working harder than ever before and taking on much more personal responsibility.

Prolonged periods of stress are not good for you. Early signs of stress can be: becoming aggressive, losing your sense of humour, sleeping badly, becoming socially withdrawn, not being able to concentrate – and, of course, starting to feel depressed. Some people even hit the bottle or take other substances.

It is vital to face up to this reality. Exercise is an excellent antidote, but many sacrifice this, saying they "don't have the time". You should also ensure that you eat properly and healthily. Comfort eating and junk food can only be bad for you. Finally, if at all possible, find time for personal quiet contemplation, or even meditation.

We all know modern society is too frenetic and it is certainly not helped by six cups of coffee in the morning and four or five alcoholic drinks in the evening. Some form of self-discipline is essential, coupled with exercise to ensure that you are in shape to handle all the pressures at work.

Managing technology so that it does not become too invasive is also a part of managing stress. Spending your whole day in front of a screen is certainly not positive. While technology can be a useful tool, some of us simply cannot switch off. Too many people – particularly the very ambitious ones – feel that they need to spend increasing time at work to show commitment. Worse, they'll send emails from home at late hours and go in to work when ill. Please – do not pick up work emails while in bed with your partner!

At the end of the day, who are you and what do you want to be? Managing stress is a crucial element in feeling good about life.

25: Admitting you are wrong

It takes a big person to accept that they are wrong, and admitting it is an important part of life.

Every leader has made mistakes. Winston Churchill got a lot of things wrong during the Second World War, but without his leadership Great Britain might never have survived.

So, where do you stand?

No one is perfect – and if you are not sure about that, try looking in the mirror.

A number of years ago I had a major row with a middle manager over some personnel issues. I then forgot about it and some ten years later, when I'd long since moved on, I bumped into him at a cocktail party where he was the host and a very senior executive. To my surprise he called me aside and apologised for both his behaviour and the fact that he was wrong all those years ago. Today he runs a large PLC and I know he commands respect – and is never afraid to admit he is wrong.

TEN TIPS ABOUT ADMITTING YOU'RE WRONG

1. Understand it's for the best.
2. Don't stress about it.
3. Do it promptly.
4. Be honest and straightforward.
5. Keep a level tone of voice.
6. Look at your audience.
7. Do not grovel.
8. See it as a stepping stone to success and commanding respect.
9. Put it behind you.
10. Do not repeat the mistake.

26: Never live on your bonus

Instead, plan for a rainy day. We read a great deal about the problems of the bonus culture and short-termism in our society. The merits or otherwise of bonuses are not a subject for this book, but what does concern me is how they affect personal lifestyle and behaviour.

Over the years I have known a number of senior people who planned their business budget in a manner that ensured they got their bonus. Besides being morally and commercially wrong, the real problem was that they depended on their bonuses to maintain their standard of living – or in plain words, they were living beyond their means.

The best advice I can give anyone is to treat a bonus as exactly that. It is a windfall you may or may not receive, depending on the year's performance. Never live on that bonus, but put it towards planning for the long term. I always set my bonus aside to help pay school fees, reduce my mortgage and plan for retirement.

I lost my job on my wedding anniversary in 1997, and it was certainly an interesting celebration that 6th November. That same year, however, I paid off the mortgage on my home and I was able to do this by utilising my prior years' bonuses to reduce the mortgage debt.

So, enjoy your bonus but don't depend on it.

27: The use and abuse of technology

Whatever has happened to gut feelings and instinct?

INFORMATION OVERLOAD – DROWNING IN DATA

Today we are bombarded with emails, voicemails, endless meaningless reports and general data clutter. It is impossible to absorb and reflect on so much information, and worse, we no longer know what is useful.

What is the information you need to make real decisions? Who needs to hear or read it? How can you simplify it within your organisation in order to improve morale – yes, it is depressing, and the quality of decision-making suffers.

I suggest an audit of what is relevant would be a good start!

ELECTRONIC COMMUNICATION

Of course, emails, smartphones and tablets etc. are an integral part of our life today. How did we survive without them? They are a wonderful "always on" way of keeping in touch with the world, but they have a hypnotic control over too many of us.

There is a simple rule in life which will protect you and could even save your career: if you feel unable to say something face to face, never put it in an email, let alone social media. Every day I read about the fallout from thoughtless tweets! Remember – once you have pressed the send button it can be very difficult to retract or erase what was said.

Sadly, many people hide behind electronic tools. While essential in the modern world, they are no substitute for a look, a tone of voice or a smile. I always believe that looking someone in the eye and speaking to them is the best way to make a judgement and determine sincerity or otherwise.

With digital media you do not have the checks and balances that you get during face-to-face interaction. You may well be in the habit of just banging off whatever comes to mind without recourse to serious thinking: this is very dangerous and could damage you badly if you get it wrong more than occasionally.

Here are some simple tips that should be borne in mind:

EMAILS

1 **Never put anything in an email that you would not want to see on the front page of a national newspaper** – a bit extreme but it makes the point.
2 **Emails should not be for negotiation, and ideally contain facts** or ask questions, and confirm what has been agreed. They should exclude personal opinions about sensitive subjects.
3 If your email does contain personal opinions, **make it clear that they are your own** and that they do not necessarily reflect the views of your company.
4 **Check when forwarding emails and edit if necessary.** I am surprised at the number of emails I receive which include two or three pages of old information which should clearly have been eliminated.
5 Last but not least, **never send an angry email (or tweet) in the heat of the moment.** Sleep on it, and in the morning, you'll have a much

clearer picture of how serious the problem really is (or isn't), and what you should do about it. This book is all about building your career, which also involves avoiding unnecessary damage.

MOBILE PHONES AND MEETINGS

I am staggered by the number of people who use their mobiles and even tablets during meetings or at dinner parties. It is almost like an addiction, and I urge you to resist the temptation. It is unnecessary (with rare exception), and is insulting to your host or to the person who is conducting the meeting.

If you are expecting an urgent phone call, request permission to take it and explain the reason.

PERSONAL TIME

Do not let emails and texting take over your personal life. Far too many people take their laptop to bed. Worse still, some even check emails while driving – which is illegal and asking for trouble.

It is important to periodically disconnect yourself from electronic communication devices, both in the office and (especially) at home. Of course, there are times when they are necessary, but if you become an addict you may end up paying a heavy personal price.

SOME USEFUL PROTOCOLS FOR PERSONAL COMMUNICATION IN OUR GLOBAL VILLAGE

We live in a global village where everything is instant. A hundred years ago, you travelled abroad on business by ship for months at a time with hardly any communication back to your family and business. Today, there is nowhere to hide, so it is more important than ever to ensure that your personal style and communication are carefully managed.

CLOUD COMPUTING AND SIMPLE MANNERS

Here is some general advice to think about when it comes to the WWW:

1 Don't post dangerous negative thoughts or anything in anger, especially in the public domain. Comments committed to the Web are almost without exception permanent: even deleted messages posted to Twitter can be found with a simple Google search.

In recent times, a number of people have lost their jobs or even ended up in court for comments made in the public domain.

2 Manage your key private thoughts. Be very careful with whom you share your innermost thoughts in the office. It's amazing how rumours fly around and grow in size!

3 Protect your identity. Safeguarding your personal "brand" online is important because employers and universities now check the social profiles of applicants. For example, if you are on Facebook and are seen misbehaving at a party, it can easily bounce back negatively, especially as more and more employers will look at your page as part of a character reference.

Good computer passwords need to be memorable and secure. A good password must be difficult to guess but easy to remember. Beware of using the names of wives, husbands and children. Hackers thrive on computer naivety.

If you do use Facebook, I suggest you block your profile to strangers.

4 If you wouldn't say it to someone's face, don't say it online. If you put something in an email or online, it can never be a secret, and you may live to regret the day.

5 A letter is still the best way to say thank you. While email and text messages have transformed the way we communicate, when it comes to expressing gratitude, the old-fashioned handwritten letter takes pride of place. A letter communicates both care and deliberation, makes everyone feel good and, as an aside, is a superb way of getting someone's attention.

If you personally adopt these tips it will stand you in surprisingly good stead in your career.

28: Who is your boss?

> *"There is only one boss. The customer. And he can fire everybody in the company from the chairman on down. Simply by spending his money somewhere else.*
> Sam Walton, founder of Walmart

It's a question that I bet you could ask a thousand people at work and never get the correct answer.

Whether a person shines shoes for a living or heads up the largest corporation in the world, the boss remains the same: it's the real customer, the consumer.

The people who work on an assembly line deep inside a big factory might think that they're working for the company that writes the pay cheque – but it is not so. They work for the person who buys the product at the end of the line; that is the person who pays everyone's salary and who decides whether a business is going to succeed or not.

Consumers don't care if a company has been around for 100 years; the minute they feel they are being treated badly, they will start putting it out of business by voting with their feet.

This boss, the real customer, the consumer, has bought or will have paid for everything you have or will have. The consumer buys all your clothes, your home and your car, pays for your children's education and finances your vocation. They pay all your bills – and in direct proportion to the way you treat them.

Some of the largest companies that had flourishing businesses a few years ago are no longer in existence. They couldn't or didn't satisfy the consumer: they forgot who the boss really was!

So doing an exceptionally good job will not only bring you joy and contentment, but also, if you appreciate that the end purpose is to satisfy consumers, it will help to generate more customers, keep those you already have, and ensure that you continue to get a pay cheque.

29: Family and friends

Too many people see work as the A to Z of their existence, so that it becomes all-consuming to the exclusion of all else. You may have financial pressures and have to work harder than you wish, but if you have any choice in the matter never forget that the most important people in your life are not in the office, but at home – your family.

Your children are only with you for a short period of time before they have lives of their own, and the relationships you build with them in their formative years will greatly influence your long-term happiness.

Likewise, never forget your real friends, because friendship is a two-way street. What you put in you get out, and if you are too busy to spend time with your friends as you climb the corporate ladder, don't expect them to welcome you with open arms when you decide to change direction or leave your career behind.

Essentially, ensure that no matter how hard you work, you have a balanced life.

30: A summary of professionalism

All of us think we're professionals – but are we?

Here is a simple checklist to help you assess how you measure up.

A professional is someone who:

- is always on time – remember, if you are not early you are late
- is always courteous and treats everyone with respect
- knows what is truly important and prioritises accordingly
- will readily get up in time to catch the early-bird flight
- accepts without complaint that jet lag comes with the job when working internationally

- explains the objective of any programme, exercise or strategy to the team and involves them in it so that they all "own the issue"
- does not blame others when problems arise, but regards problems and failure as shared responsibility
- does not let their ego get the better of them and knows the price of a pint of beer or a litre of petrol
- parks in the right place and not those reserved for customers – unless, of course, they are a customer
- thanks people, whether or not they are "just doing their job"
- looks people in the eye and speaks clearly, rather than muttering, looking down and fiddling with an electronic device; everyone wants to be appreciated
- doesn't check their phone in the middle of a conversation
- is bound by their word (old-fashioned, but of inestimable value)
- is always willing to help other people improve their own capability and career development
- knows that a job title is purely a title and a means to an end, not an end in itself
- learns from everybody – young or old – and respects the wisdom of those who have gone before, done it the hard way and, in fact, have made many mistakes from which others can learn
- realises that we all have one mouth and two ears, and that it is up to us to listen more often
- does not abuse technology and ensures that phones, etc. are turned off in all meetings (unless there is an absolute emergency for which prior permission is sought)
- is always neatly dressed with clean shoes and a tidy appearance
- is wary about office gossip and never character-assassinates people within the organisation
- recognises that you have to fail sometimes in order to succeed and that each failure is a valuable lesson
- appreciates that business is cyclical in the long term, and as a society, we will continue to go through recessions from time to time

- thinks long- and short-term. Yes, there are always short-term needs (e.g. we need to feed our families), so if you are going to build a great company, think and act long-term after addressing day-to-day activities efficiently and effectively.

If you can tick off 90% of these points, that's great (I prefer 100%, of course); less than 90% and you need to look in the mirror and do some self-correction.

BASIC FINANCIAL LOGIC

The only unforgivable sin in business is to run out of cash.
Harold Geneen, businessman

31: Turnover – profit and cash

In this age of preoccupation with short-term bonuses, far too many big-company executives worry about turnover and immediate profit. Small companies are usually more realistic, for they are concerned with the most important issue: cash.

Remember the cliché: turnover is for vanity, profit is for sanity, but only cash is reality.

If the turnover is good, I would assume there is a good profit margin. But a profit margin is not in itself cash; it is usually the promise of future cash, assuming your debtors pay you and you are able to settle your creditors. Real profit is really the generation of sustainable cash. After all, it's no good owning a Ferrari if you can't afford to put petrol in the tank. You can't bank turnover or profit, only cash!

When I look at companies, I try to assess the style and focus of the Chief Executive, along with the company's ability to generate sufficient cash in order to sustain growth and build a long-term future. I'm always nervous when I see share prices rise dramatically because of rumours and stories in the marketplace. Long-term sustainable growth underpinned by good cash generation is crucial.

32: Some useful ways to manage cash flow

1. All staff should have a sense of cash responsibility. This means **all** staff and not just the credit-control department. If, for example, you are in the sales force, you should want to know when your customers will pay for the goods they purchase.
2. Check the creditworthiness of new customers. Selling is one thing, being paid is another. Carefully check the creditworthiness of new customers and watch settlement trends with old ones. This is even more important in a recession than during good times. Far too many firms collapse because they have good sales but cannot collect their outstandings.
3. Invoices should be dispatched promptly. Send out invoices immediately after delivering the goods or providing a service. This is elementary, but many companies delay before sending out invoices. Prompt invoicing is sound business practice and essential to your future.
4. Good credit control requires discipline. Negotiate the best payment terms with your suppliers as early as possible. Rigorously chase overdue invoices and put bad payers on COD (cash on

delivery). Take advantage of early payment discounts if you have the cash, and conversely make sure companies don't abuse your payment terms. Examine ways to stagger payment for large expensive items, e.g. plant and machinery are often payable over many months. Consider factoring your sales book (which essentially means handing over your debtors for someone else to collect); while it will cost you money, it can be useful in helping you manage cash-flow shortages.

5 Manage your daily cash. Everyone should be able to pay in cash and cheques on the same day as they are received. It is amazing how many small companies are lax in this area. Managing your money means not only paying in cash, but also ensuring you obtain the best possible interest on the money sitting in the bank. Use internet banking whenever possible as it will save you considerable time (there is nothing worse than standing in long queues) – time which could be more effectively utilised in managing your business.

6 Seek government financial support wherever possible. In these difficult times, most governments offer some sort of support for small businesses be they grants or special loans, etc. You should look into all the possibilities offered by governments and other bodies.

To summarise using a golf analogy: drive for show and putt for dough. We love to see a wonderful 250-yard drive but, of course, it's not more important than a 9-inch putt: each counts as one stroke. It's how you finish that matters.

But how does this apply to business? Well, we all love sales and we all love profit, but what about cash collection – the boring job of bringing in the money? It's exactly the same as putting – it is essential to keep your business in perspective.

If you grow too quickly, you will usually have cash problems. If you do not collect your cash, you will certainly run into trouble. So whatever you do when you are running a business, make sure that your credit control and cash collection are focused and always a priority, and that everyone in the business appreciates this logic.

33: Working with suppliers

1. **Brief them properly.** They need to know what you want, when you need it and how much you're willing to pay.
2. **You are the customer.** There's a thin line between a supplier and a friend. Make sure you draw it. That makes it hard for them to resort to emotional blackmail if things go wrong. And don't go soft on them; make sure any mistakes are reflected in the invoice.
3. **Harness their brain power.** Markets change, new suppliers spring up and prices fall. Contact them periodically for an update on industry developments. Ask how these changes could be used to improve their service and your products and ask for any other ideas they may have.
4. Are they really your best suppliers? **Review your suppliers' performance** and get quotes from their rivals.
5. **Don't rely on one person.** You need to know who is behind your point of contact or you could be in trouble if they are away or, worse, leave your supplier.
6. **Be generous and courteous.** If your supplier does a good job, let them know and encourage them. Be prepared to be a positive referee for them within the industry.

When I was the Chief Executive of IDV UK (now part of Diageo), I convened a conference of all our suppliers, where we presented to them an outline of our strategic plans for the next five years. I believe that there are few secrets in this world and, while of course they were also supplying competitors, I saw this as the key to our success. It provided them with a clearly understood roadmap of our plans – and, more importantly, entailed working with people internally and externally.

We had a vigorous Q&A debate at the end, followed by a splendid lunch. The feedback was superb, and led to us tweaking our strategy to build a much stronger and more effective relationship with our suppliers thereafter, to mutual advantage.

RETAILING

In the factory we make cosmetics. In the store we sell hope.
Charles Revson, founder of Revlon.

34: Fundamental principles of retailing

I started my career at the age of fourteen, working part-time in retail stores, and when I was twenty-two, I worked for the Spar retail group in South Africa. A large part of my job then was to convince middle-aged conservative shop owners, who mostly had counter-service stores, that the future lay in self-service. As a young man with little experience, that was a difficult challenge at the time. This is hard to believe today when we are now dealing with the internet and armchair shopping.

There is a great deal of commentary about the demise of the high street and retailers facing a difficult future. Of course, if you act like an ostrich, burying your head in the sand and not observing or responding to the changing environment, you will be in trouble. On the other hand, innovation always brings opportunities, and if you are in retail, it is your job to respond positively to changing consumer expectations.

The essence of retailing has always been about being able to see, smell, touch and experience the goods in front of you, but there are issues today with armchair internet shopping.

There are essentially three types of shoppers that need to be recognised: experiential, functional and convenience shoppers. Your job is to identify them and respond accordingly.

Experiential is essentially a term which suggests there is a total shopping experience involving entertainment, restaurants, coffee shops, lunch venues and who knows what else. The purchase of specific goods is only part of the experience and, for some people (particularly those living alone), social interaction is a major objective of the process.

Functional, of course, is buying precisely what you need, which may be basic food (your weekly shop), new batteries, razor blades or other specific items.

Convenience is exactly that. If you drive, is there parking available? Is it free? Are the stores easy to reach? And if you are shopping for a range of goods, is there sufficient variety?

All of this is now strongly influenced by the internet, and different customers shop in multiple ways. They may visit stores, they may read the reviews of the stores and the offerings, and they may well make online comparisons, and many now shop online. Sometimes they even do this on their phones while out in the high street!

Wise retailers recognise that actual stores have to be integrated with websites and internet comparison shopping. They must also, of course, always be conscious of the influence of social media.

A good retailer has to be multifaceted. Even if a store or stores are based on the high street, one must positively accept the conundrum of doing business through the internet because online shopping is here to stay and growing as a percentage of trade year by year.

LOYALTY PROGRAMMES

More and more retailers are offering loyalty programmes as a way of not only encouraging you to support the company's retail outlets, but also as a way of tracking and analysing purchases and trends etc. Further, personal one-to-one relationships are being established between suppliers and customers at home via both electronic and printed communication, e.g. "Dear Mrs Jones, in return for your loyalty, we're giving you a voucher for…" Most major airlines have been doing this for many years, and these programmes often make the customer feel appreciated and thus more loyal.

35: Retail is detail

Raymond Ackerman, the founder of Pick n Pay (the number-one retail food chain in South Africa), built his empire on four fundamental principles, which he describes in his 2010 book, *A Sprat to Catch a Mackerel*.

These are: merchandise, people, marketing and administration.

It's a philosophy I have always supported and all four principles are essential for a balanced and successful retail operation.

Clearly, you have to have exciting merchandise (the product or services offered), so in this context, how are you going to make money from offering them?

1. How is your merchandise displayed and your service offered? When you walk into any store, remember the old cliché, "eye level is buy level". How do you make your offering stand out? How do you compare with competitors and what makes you different? Where applicable, how much stock is needed to keep the business going

forward? Can you finance it? How will you cope with the downturns that happen from time to time? The same principle, of course, applies to the internet figuratively.

2. Ackerman rightly focused strongly on the people in the company. The ideal employee is one who acts as if it is their own business. The John Lewis Partnership in the UK stresses this aspect very publicly; all employees are shareholders. How, then, do you best motivate and reward those employees? How many will be needed, since they are often one's greatest overhead? Who will help you to ensure that their needs are consistently being met as the business grows, so that the team being built is a great one?

3. Marketing, in the broadest sense, is vital not only in order to bring customers to your business, but to keep them interested in and wanting to shop with you, be it in-store or online.

    Spending marketing money is easy, but spending it wisely, with clear objectives, is much more difficult. How can you stretch your budget to maximise impact and interest with the target community?

    Never forget that there is also a social responsibility, and if you work in a local area, make sure you are part of that community. For example, a good friend of mine has an eponymously named estate agency. He has built up a great business over the last thirty years, not least because his company supports many local community activities and he is always visible at local events. This creates a very good image for his agency. Good social responsibility is invariably linked to long-term self-interest!

4. Finally, make sure that you have very sound administration and fiscal control. How do you plan your cash flow? How do you budget for salaries, supplier payments, taxes and general outflow? How do you keep control of sales and costs without undue expenditure? Without efficient control and administration your business will run into serious trouble. Ultimately, if you do not pay your suppliers on time or your staff each month, you will lose everything you have worked for over the years.

It is a well-known cliché that no one ever went broke because they had too much cash. Retail certainly is detail; forget this at your peril.

SIMPLE MARKETING LOGIC

The twenty-first century is seeing new forms of marketing, driven by the internet, online shopping etc. and the High Street under increasing pressure. Never forget, however, that it is the product that always forms the future of marketing, as it has always done.

PERCEPTION IS REALITY.

36: What is marketing?

There are many definitions of marketing and I don't intend to create a new one, but if a company is to succeed it has to provide the ultimate consumers with what they want, thus satisfying their needs at a price which they regard as appropriate and which will allow the company to make a profit.

One simple definition I rather like is that marketing is about "improving the standard of living for all". If you think about it, the greatest progress in society has always come about when marketing has been allowed to flourish. The dynamic growth in Asia and China in recent years particularly confirms this point.

Mankind is entrepreneurial by nature, and since time began people have produced goods, for sale to others. The more successful were those that offered the best goods at attractive prices. This might be a small stall at the side of the road, a retail shop or a multinational business servicing the globe. As you progress, so the positioning and importance of your brand and brand identity become critical.

What is fundamental is never to forget that consumers will decide on your future (see "Who is your boss?"), and it is your job to ensure that your brand or brands are always relevant to their lives.

In so doing, reflect on every aspect of your product, from its creation and use to its packaging and image, and all the processes that ultimately move your brand from source to final destination.

MARKETING IS AT THE HEART OF EVERYTHING

Brands accompany you on your journey through life. Over time, brand attributes and quality impressions register in your brain, which influences your purchase decisions.

Successful companies are those that keep ahead of the dynamically changing global marketplace. Today's customers are much more sophisticated and ready to challenge brands on offer, and with consumer goods often being similar, establishing clear-cut differentiation is no easy task.

Marketing-orientated companies are those that harness their activities to provide customers and consumers with superb perceived value. They have an organisational culture which is flexible and "intrapreneurial" (that is, it encourages employees to behave like entrepreneurs while working within a large organisation), and they realise that brands have to meet ever-changing consumer needs and perceptions.

What do you think of Coca-Cola v. Pepsi? Or Mercedes v. BMW or Jaguar? Or Microsoft, Google and Apple?

Good companies meet consumer needs now, but *great* companies look ahead to match their offering to tomorrow's requirements.

KNOW YOUR COMPETITORS

Some companies are sadly so inward-looking and self-absorbed that they forget to take cognisance of what their competitors are doing – with dangerous consequences. Hopefully this well-known story makes the point:

Some years ago, a couple were walking through the bush in Zimbabwe. Noticing a lion behind them, the pair stopped suddenly. One quietly opened her rucksack and pulled out a pair of running shoes. Her partner observed, 'That won't help you at all – you can't run faster than a lion.' 'I don't have to,' she retorted. 'I just have to run faster than you!'

37: Intrinsic and extrinsic variables

Like it or not, we are all influenced by packaging and presentation, and when it comes to consumer goods, we increasingly shop at self-service stores, supermarkets and now online. The presentation online or on the shelf, the pricing and, of course, the image of the brand will influence our purchase decisions.

Some hundred years ago, when someone bought sugar, it was stored in a sack, then weighed and put into a brown paper bag and handed over to them. The **intrinsic** offering is the fundamental product; it provided **intrinsic** satisfaction in that the customer bought the non-branded sugar to satisfy their needs.

With modern marketing, in most parts of the world, sugar today is sold in attractive packaging and branded. Like it or not, you are influenced by your perception of the brand.

Essentially, this means that it is not only the packaging, but all the imagery created by the marketer which leads you to feel good about that purchase. That is its **extrinsic** value.

People will pay a premium price for products which they want, and this is why there is a luxury goods market. This concept is, of course, particularly relevant in the world of fashion and haute couture. As the fashion designer Karl Lagerfeld succinctly put it, "We created a product nobody needs, but people want."

VODKA

This is probably one of the best products to help explain the concept of intrinsic and extrinsic. Vodka is supposed to be odourless, tasteless and colourless. Usually made from grain, molasses, grape or potato spirit, vodka is heavily filtered and cleaned through activated charcoal and other processes. It is very difficult to tell the difference between one vodka and another and, if you add ice and cola, almost impossible.

So why would you pay £10 or less for a cheap vodka, £15 for a vodka like Smirnoff, £20 for Absolut, £30 for Grey Goose and a lot more for some of the niche vodkas on the market?

The answer is that perception is reality, and the marketers of those vodkas have spent millions on creating the image associated with their brands. This leads consumers to feel comfortable paying a lot more for their chosen brand because of all the extrinsic elements and the "feel-good factors" related to that purchase.

Indeed, research has shown that the more expensive brands may well be regarded as better value in the mind of the consumer.

BMW V. FORD

Here is another example to toy with. I will not comment on the merits of either brand, but if you were given the choice of a BMW saloon car with a Ford engine inside, or a Ford equivalent saloon car with a BMW engine inside, both at the same price, which one would you choose?

Ferrari is blunt in its assessment of the motor market: "We don't sell a normal product – we sell a dream."

CONCLUSION

Your job as a marketer is always to ensure that the intrinsic qualities of your brand are superb but equally – if not more importantly – that all the various extraneous extrinsic factors create an image of the brand to justify the price paid and to build long-term loyalty.

A former CEO of Coca-Cola summarised this philosophy thus: "A brand is essentially a promise – a great brand is a promise kept!"

38: Marketing myopia

Some fifty years ago, one of the original teachers of modern marketing, the late Theodore Levitt, wrote a wonderful article entitled *Marketing Myopia*, which I studied as a student. He suggested that not enough companies truly understand what business they are in and he used examples from the rail, film and petroleum industries to illustrate the point.

Many early movie producers thought they were in the film business as opposed to being in the entertainment business, and so did not see television as competition – and how wrong were they? Likewise, many people in the petroleum business did not see gas as competition, but of course, both belong to the fuel business. With the concern about global warming today and electric cars etc, what next?

The example I like best is the railroad industry. In nineteenth-century USA, some wealthy people left railroad stock in perpetuity to their families – a great financial mistake. Railway transport declined rapidly, superseded mostly by road and air. They simply did not understand that they were in the transport business and that their job was to recognise that the consumer wanted to get from A to B as comfortably and rapidly and/or cost efficiently as possible, by whatever means made the most sense.

Reflect for a moment on the dynamic growth of mobile telecommunications in recent years and the swings and roundabouts experienced by companies such as Nokia, BlackBerry and Apple, and the point should be very clear.

Successful companies are targeted by their competitors, and you cannot for a moment rest on your laurels. In a shrinking – if not shrunken – global village, competitors are always seeking to make your brand obsolete, especially with modern technology.

So my advice is this: think carefully about your business and make sure you truly understand your competition and where it is going, as well as how relevant your brand or brands are to tomorrow's world.

39: Maslow's Hierarchy of Needs

This is a psychological theory, proposed by Abraham Maslow in his 1943 paper, *A Theory of Human Motivation*. Maslow subsequently extended the idea to include his observations of humans' innate curiosity. His theories parallel many others concerning human developmental psychology, all of which focus on describing the stages of growth in humans.

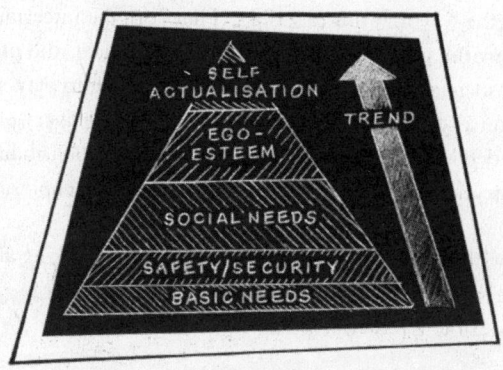

It's a useful marketing tool, so let me describe Maslow in language that relates to that field.

The bottom rung, "Basic Needs", discusses just that – the most basic needs of primitive mankind. Once these needs are satisfied and you have a family and a roof above your head, the next need is "Safety/Security", which implies looking after your family and what you have. We then move to a sense of belonging, which Maslow termed "Love Needs" and I call "Social Needs". Man is a social animal; we all like to mix with people and interact – with rare exception – and this is where friendship and families, the bedrock of our existence, are all-important.

As our standard of living improves, so we become influenced more and more by brands, and – as part of our social interaction and personal satisfaction – the brands we purchase become increasingly important. This is where what Maslow described as "Esteem" and I term "Ego" come in. Remember my vodka analogy?

Most people in the developed and the developing world operate in the Social Esteem and Ego arenas, which are essentially about striving to better their standard of living and to have this improved status noticed by peers. You, as a marketer, must ensure that your brands are packaged, positioned and delivered to meet their needs.

The top rung in Maslow's pyramid, Self-Actualisation, is not often a major part of marketing thinking, for very few people are totally fulfilled in the way that this describes. That said, the uncertainty in today's world, plus thoughts on morality, prejudice, and other important societal elements come more and more into play, so perhaps you also should reflect on this rung in the delivery of your brands. Indeed, a sense of social conscience and responsibility to the planet is increasingly important for more and more people, and thus brands.

Maslow's hierarchy is a useful tool to use when thinking about your brands and the position they are in.

From Maslow, a few concluding comments:

- Products are made by companies.
- Brands, however, are made and indeed owned by people – the consumers.
- Brands are living entities, and the image of a brand is subjective, as it depends on the eye of the beholder.
- A brand's image and perception must be constantly refreshed with consumers over the long haul.
- How valuable is your brand? Sell it and you will soon know.

40: The life cycle of a brand manager

The great brands of the world take time to build. If you have a winning formula, change it at your peril.

Of course, your brand must always be relevant, but many of the great brand campaigns of the world last for many years (with slight modifications). Likewise, the core elements of your packaging should not be changed too often.

I always worry about the new brand manager or advertising executive who thinks that the way to make an impression is to change the packaging or the campaign, or even introduce unnecessary range extensions. Are they really thinking about the brand, or more about how they can get promotion or a short-term bonus? So, the life cycle of an over-ambitious brand manager could look like this: repackage, relaunch – boom! Resign!

I was heavily involved in the growth of Baileys Irish Cream in its formative years during the 1970s and '80s. I saw one of my main roles as ensuring that the packaging, product and positioning (thus the brand) were always consistent, so we didn't have too many different advertising campaigns – and we certainly never positioned Baileys as a frivolous drink; we would never, for example, suggest pouring it over ice cream (as I know sometimes happens).

How people drink Baileys in their homes is their business – it is a light liqueur, enjoyed in many different ways. In the early stages, though, no one quite understood the brand, so we always positioned it in a serious manner.

On an intrinsic level, because cream and alcohol are not natural bedfellows and tend to separate more easily in hot climates, we took the major decision to change the formula to ensure that this didn't happen. The trade-off was that Baileys was not mixable, but this suited our purpose by making the intrinsic product reliable and stable, and we could therefore safely attach the concept that this was a drink for serious appreciation on its own merits.

Today it is the world's number one liqueur, with annual sales in the region of seven million cases.

The message is simple: yes, change is necessary at times, but don't allow it to happen at the whim of a new brand manager or advertising agency executive trying to boost their career.

I'll leave a question on the table: is Baileys being stretched too much with too many new flavours?

41: The consumer does not have a financial year

In the short-term bonus culture of recent years, far too many executives are only interested in selling their goods to their customers (e.g. the retailers) with little regard to the consumers at the end of the chain. They focus on their short-term goals, like getting a bonus or a promotion. This often results in the trade being overloaded with stock and, consequently, the customer having to cut the price, with a resultant negative impact on the brand.

I have been horrified at times to find that people selling in the field were virtually dumping stock in order to make short-term targets. They had no real thought or concern for the image of the brand or for the potential damage from their actions.

> When I was the President of United Distillers North America during the recession of the 1990s, we had 100% distribution for Johnnie Walker in the marketplace. I was, however, criticised for refusing to sell in more stock. I knew doing so would be a very dangerous short-term practice; not only will you risk damaging your brand, but you will probably have to give extra credit because of the unnecessary, extra-large purchases retailers will have to make.

We all want to sell in as much as possible, but it should be only what is genuinely required to meet the needs of the consumers frequenting the stores in question.

You want to maximise the shelf space that your brands occupy and enjoy the most prominent display positions in the shops (such as the "gondola ends", at the ends of the aisles), but only if it is a logical part of an integrated marketing and selling plan.

THE SALT STORY AND "SELLING THROUGH"

Let me tell you a little parable about salt.

Many years ago, I walked into a small store in the country and I couldn't see the woman behind the counter because of all the bags of salt stacked in front of her. I said to her, 'Madam, you must sell a lot of salt!' and she replied, 'No, I don't sell a lot of salt, but the gentleman that sold it to me – he sure sells a lot of it.'

I hope this simple message is clear: your job is not just to sell to, but to sell through the trade channels and to help your customers successfully provide the consumers with what they want.

It is never a real sale until your customers have sold the goods you sold to them and have re-ordered. Then you know you are starting to build your brand, as well as a relationship with your partners and trade customers. The only good sale is a repeat purchase!

42: Effective selling

Customers do not buy your brands because you are a large company with a global presence. They are – rightly – only interested in what is in it for them. Your past may reflect a great history and be a form of guarantee, but your job is to meet current and future needs.

When meeting customers, think of a few simple points:

1. Are you genuinely able to help solve your customer's problems?
2. Who talks more – you or the customer? It should be the latter and, strangely enough, the more your customer talks, the better they will usually think you are.
3. Ask lots of questions to dig deeper and find out what your customer's true needs are.

4 Listen carefully to answers without interrupting.
5 Remember the acronym WAIT – Why Am I Talking?
6 Last but not least, your word should be your bond, because one sale is simply that: one sale. If you are wise, you will want to build a long-term relationship, with regular, hopefully increasing sales.

DISCOUNTING: A DANGEROUS PRACTICE

In today's challenging retail environment, the impulse to discount and sell volume is understandable when all around are doing so, but never forget that most discounting comes at a cost. Price promotions destroy brand image and commodify them, undoing the good work that has gone into giving the consumer a reason to buy beyond functionality.

You have to balance short-term profit and long-term brand equity, and price is undeniably a basic component of a brand's image.

So, before you rush to discount your brand, think of the advice given to me by Hugh Burkitt, former Chief Executive of The Marketing Society:

"Sales promotion is the sex, drugs and rock and roll of marketing – highly enjoyable, often effective in the short term, but dangerous to the user and very difficult to control once the habit has started."

43: Everyone is involved in marketing

Marketing and brand-building are not solely the responsibility of the marketing department. As mentioned earlier, your only true boss is the consumer, and everyone in your company should appreciate that they have a role to play in the marketing process. It is up to the leaders of the company to ensure that this is effectively communicated because, if your brands are not successful, there will be no company, and thus no jobs.

It is important to accept that people throughout the company may have ideas to improve brands and processes, and this should be encouraged. It is also no bad thing to reward in some tangible form those who have made an improvement to the ultimate benefit of the brands themselves.

Every single aspect of the business has an impact on marketing at some stage or another and this needs to be appreciated, communicated and positively recognised.

WHITE DIAMOND V. MAINSTAY

In the 1970s, when I was working for the South African arm of IDV as their Marketing Director, I played cricket for the company in a match against a local club side. Our team included people from different departments, including two who worked in the factory.

After the match I bought a round of drinks in the bar, ordering White Diamond cane spirit, our company brand.

To my surprise, one of the production people asked for a Mainstay – the brand leader belonging to our major competitor. When I challenged him on it, he replied, 'I work in production; I have nothing to do with marketing.'

I saw this as a failure on our part as senior management, and on the following Monday I set up communication meetings to talk to all company personnel about how everyone can be a brand ambassador.

Every employee of your company should have an understanding of your brands and an obvious loyalty to them and the company. If you cannot command company brand-loyalty, how can you expect to win over consumers at large?

INTERNAL MARKETING

In any organisation, people try to convince others to do certain things or support ideas in order to get the desired results. This is a natural part of life. When a person meets someone in whom they're interested, they will try to put their best foot forward and create the right impression. This is basic personal marketing. Some are good at it, while others are not. But everyone learns from experience and can improve.

In virtually all companies, far too little time and effort is spent on helping people to improve the quality of internal communications and negotiation, with the result that far too much negative energy is used. We should all think carefully about how we market our messages, what the end objective is and how best to get there.

If you are going to succeed in business, you must strive to be a better internal marketer. If there's one thing to be sure of, it's that there will be many road blocks on the way that you'll have to try to overcome through your communication and effective marketing skills.

44: The key to good marketing communication

I am often bemused by creative advertising that wins awards because of supposed creative brilliance. Sadly, all too often the brilliance is about winning awards and not customers. Surely everything should be directed to winning customers and then retaining their loyalty.

THE ROLE OF ADVERTISING IN A NUTSHELL
Advertising in its various forms is about establishing a long-term, positive relationship with the consumer.

To quote the great David Ogilvy in his 1955 talk on brand image:

> *The manufacturers who dedicate their advertising to building the most favourable image, the most sharply defined personality for their brand, are the ones who will get the largest share of these markets at the highest profit – in the long run ... The time has come to sound an alarm, to warn our clients what is going to happen to their brands if they spend so much on deals that there is no money left for advertising to build their brand ... Deals don't build the kind of indestructible image which is the only thing that can make your brand part of the fabric of the American life.*

Some fifty years ago, when I was first a student of marketing, I learnt a very simple formula about advertising and communication which has stood the test of time: AIDA.

No, I'm not talking about Verdi's opera, but a simple route map to good communication, supposedly formulated by the American advertising guru E. St Elmo Lewis in 1908.

1. First you must gain a customer's **Attention**; a bold headline that moves you straight on to...
2. **Interest** – aroused by reading or listening to or seeing the advertisement.
3. At this stage, if the ad is working properly it will create **Desire**.
4. If it is an effective advertisement, it should now lead to **Action** – which is to close the sale.

Next time you look at an advertisement, think about this simple guideline, which I hope will also be useful to you in your career.

Here's another little tip to help you present yourself: KISS – or Keep It Short, Stupid.

In conjunction with AIDA, it is appropriate to recognise that modern consumers have a very short attention span, as they are constantly bombarded with marketing messages. This reinforces the value of KISS. I know this well because this is the advice my wife gives me whenever I am called upon to make a speech.

EMAIL BRANDING: A LOST OPPORTUNITY

We know that most written communication today is via email. What surprises me then is how few emails are branded – what a waste that is of a good brand-building and communications opportunity!

It is very simple to have an email heading (which can also incorporate updates and other points of interest), yet few companies bother to do so. At the very least, put a meaningful heading in the subject line that will be relevant to the reader. I also sign off business emails with my phone number and website details.

Why don't you ensure that your company – and maybe even your department – has a suitable email heading at the top of every piece of electronic communication?

After all, a formal letter from your company is always on headed notepaper, so why should an email be different?

45: Get out of your ivory tower and meet the real customers

In a world of large business and increasing bureaucracy, far too many executives spend more time in their offices than is necessary. We have become very good shufflers of paper and email fanatics. However, what we forget is that it is ultimately the consumer who votes with his or her feet and the customer who influences the consumer.

Management by walkabout is, as I mentioned earlier, not just about being seen on the office floor, but also strongly about getting out to meet your real customers. I am thus a great believer in using shoe leather.

In other words, you must get out into the trade. It is easy to be aloof and dictate and to rely on others as you climb the corporate ladder, but you **must** meet your customers. You must see the people who really buy your products.

During fifty years of selling international brands, wherever I went I always spent at least a day in the field on every trip in every major city. If you don't travel much, at least set time in your diary to visit customers. If you don't put it in the diary and make it a part of your life, it will not happen. It is amazing how other things take over.

CUSTOMERS COME FROM ALL WALKS OF LIFE

I have been fortunate to have had an enjoyable career in the liquor industry, and I have met with virtually every single stratum of society in my time. People who enjoy quality alcohol range from royalty down to very humble people in tiny villages all over the world.

Using my industry as an example, when you travel, you must not just focus on the five-star hotels and the quality liquor stores, but should visit people in all walks of life in their own settings, including seedy night clubs and tiny shops. Meet as many different types of customers as possible – talk to them, ask questions, take an interest in them and earn their respect. You will learn a great deal.

You may be marketing a very successful brand, but brands have to be constantly refreshed and kept in a state of good repair, and it is our job as executives to keep close to those consumers and thus in touch with reality. Remember: it is the consumer who decides your future.

RELATIONSHIP MANAGEMENT AND YOUR CUSTOMERS

En route to the consumer, it is essential to build lasting relationships with loyal customers in the trade – your route to market. This is a key part of effective trade marketing. I don't mean wining and dining your customers (although this happens from time to time) but by ensuring you are focused on a few simple fundamentals:

- Deliver the best possible service and superb value. As you travel around, reflect on your relationship with hotels and why you prefer A to B. Then revert back to your own business. How good is your service?
- Do your customers trust you? Is your word your bond?
- Do you continually look for new ways to help your customers? Think about ways to build ongoing loyalty. Amongst others, you may consider long-term financial incentives.
- Do you audit customer defections to understand what went wrong and what you can do better in the future? It costs considerably more to attract new customers than to keep existing ones.
- Do you really have a good sales force?

While everyone in the company should be marketing-orientated, your sales force is usually the primary contact with your customer. It may be the field sales force or the telesales force and ironically, on a positive/negative, the credit-control department. I mention the latter because, in their difficult role, they have an important impact on the future relationship with your customers.

Ensure that your sales force is properly trained, not only about the company and its brands, but also on the importance of good interpersonal relationships – soft skills. Volume may be useful, but it is really about profitable sales, recognising short and long-term goals.

A good sales executive is a self-starter, often working from home and thus has a strong sense of planning and time management. They clearly recognise that customers are busy, are on time for meetings, are focused, and know that their job is to help the customers through the selling of their brands.

It is management's job to lead, motivate and integrate the sales force. What you don't want to hear are some of these all too familiar comments:

- 'I haven't seen a sales representative for weeks.'
- 'I noticed that Li is telling my buyer that he is looking for another job.'
- 'Smith clearly had a heavy night last night.'
- 'Jones seems very bored and uninterested when she calls on us.'
- 'Your service is so bad that I think I'll switch suppliers.'

So, visit your customers and find out how they feel about your sales team versus the competition. It is amazing what you can learn when you get out of your office!

46: The 80:20 rule for good businesses

80% of our time should be spent on wooing the customer and 20% on internal process. Unfortunately, as companies grow and become more bureaucratic, these ratios change negatively. The ultimate bureaucrat is, of course, government, but globally we are at last seeing a crackdown on top-heavy bureaucratic incompetence. At least, I hope so.

In most large organisations, too much time is spent on internal processes – simply getting the daily job done. It may be trying to convince another department to take an interest in or take responsibility for a project, when the department in question is not interested because the project was not their idea. It may be because of egos and politics.

Size also has a role to play and sometimes, in very large companies, executives and staff forget that the purpose of the company is to win consumers and build a long-term future. Unfortunately, for some people it's purely about making regular income without understanding how the company's success is the key to the future. In some cases, the company is simply "a life support system for the ego".

Watch for any danger signals in your company. If you can help to improve the situation, then great! If not, and if you see deviation from the 80:20 rule as impeding real progress, it may be time to look elsewhere.

47: Creativity, innovation and new brand development

Creativity and innovation apply to all parts of the business and should be nurtured and encouraged. You should tap into all the talent in the organisation because you never know from where a good idea will emerge.

In some companies, creative people operate as if they exist in a vacuum and are not part of the real world. Great creativity is essential, but it must be harnessed to business logic.

I'm going to focus on brand and product innovation and how I see creativity working best, based on my own experience.

HARNESSING AND MANAGING CREATIVE TALENT

True competitive advantage comes from creative insights that translate into the brands of the future. Selling and marketing the same as others is guaranteed to lead to the commercial graveyard. Great companies encourage "intrapreneurial" thinking.

Managing and harnessing mavericks may not always be easy, but they are essential. A good intrapreneur (an entrepreneurial spirit working within an organisation) is inspirational but goal orientated, happy to challenge convention and creative and tenacious. Often the greatest enemy to potential new brands is internal bureaucracy and NIH (Not Invented Here). Great organisations understand the need to encourage creative insights to drive them to think and do things differently. It saddens me to see how negative a lot of management is to lateral creative thinking.

It is important to realise that building companies and brands is a marathon and not a sprint and one must do the basics well. You may have a head of innovation or new product development, but that person must be part of a team and there needs to be a proper process to screen ideas, which are either rejected or moved further along the development chain.

INNOVATION REQUIRES PEOPLE TO MAKE DECISIONS

I am of the view that innovation will never succeed if it is decided upon by a committee. At best, committees are full of Dr Nos and silent bureaucrats (just think of some governments!). On the other hand, I do believe in an advisory board to express opinions on each and every project and give you advice – but they should not have voting rights.

Innovation can be a lonely process, so it's important that you have support from above and that you have positive colleagues/peers to act as good sounding boards.

When I was Head of Global Marketing at IDV in the 1970s, I had a wonderful colleague in charge of New Product Development named Tom Jago. His invention, Baileys Irish Cream, actually failed in research, but he believed so strongly in the brand and its potential that he hid the results.

When I started working with Tom, my job was to protect him at board level and to focus on the commercial aspects of what he was doing. We launched Malibu and other brands together, with help from our advisors but opposition from the Dr Nos and negative thinkers, who seemed to be everywhere.

With input and support from our advisors, we kept a running list of the top twenty ideas we thought worthy of consideration. We met quarterly and revised the list, removing some and adding others so that there was always a pipeline of new projects, a number of which subsequently became successful brands.

It is always easier to say no than yes, especially as most new brands tend to fail. Equally, they are the lifeblood of a company and innovation must be fostered and supported by top management

This was fundamentally important for Tom and me; the innovative culture of the company meant that we were encouraged to create and to get out and try things. I am nervous in the current environment, where the larger the company, the more everything is researched, with instinct and gut feeling too often ignored.

"IF YOU SEE A GOOD IDEA, STEAL IT"

Last but not least, as you travel around the world you may see an idea which will lead you to a new brand. I don't mean you should literally steal ideas, but that you should be receptive to concepts that give you indications of what can be achieved if you change things and do it right. You may learn from a product or a process, and adopting, adapting and improving has merit.

It is said that this is exactly what the Japanese motor industry did in the 1960s and 1970s, improving dramatically on the technology that was only moving slowly forward in the USA and Europe. In more recent times, the Chinese have been extremely active in this area. Yes, there are moral issues at stake, and I am totally opposed to people who steal trademarks and technology, but at the same time, if you see a good idea and can improve on it, and be truly innovative, why not?

THE TRUE ORIGIN OF MALIBU

The idea for Malibu came from the United States, and a failed brand called Coco Ribe that had a coconut rum flavour. The Head of Marketing for IDV South Africa purchased a bottle of Coco Ribe on one of his trips to the USA, took it home with him and created a brand called Coco Rico, in a hand-painted white bottle with distinctive graphics.

At that time (the late 1970s), South Africa was one of the pariah nations of the world because of apartheid; the future President Mandela – that wonderful world statesman – was still languishing in prison. We were convinced Coco Rico had a good future, but for all the obvious reasons there was a lot of opposition in London and elsewhere. So we renamed it Malibu, imported the initial consignment from South Africa, used the same packaging and bottled it in Harlow, Essex. We did not research it and we told no one where it came from. However, we had an internal problem to deal with: negative colleagues.

In order to convince them that Malibu was worthy of serious consideration, I flew to Boston to meet the great Ted Levitt, who was lecturing on the subject of Marketing at Harvard Business School. I invited him and his wife to join us for a weekend in the Bahamas where we were having our first ever global new product conference. Levitt liked the Malibu idea and, as he was the moderator at our conference, doubting Thomases were muted in their objections and then agreed that we should launch the brand.

We called it Malibu, "Caribbean-style rum", and we launched through night clubs and selected bottle stores and bars with an advertising and marketing campaign using the headline: "It comes from Paradise and tastes like Heaven."

It was an immediate success and is today owned by Pernod Ricard, with sales of over four million cases per annum.

> From the beginning, people thought it was a Caribbean drink and, as it happens, today there is a large Malibu distillery in Barbados, which is now its formal home. A strange turnaround!

48: Product life cycle and growing too fast

Very rarely do new brands take off at dramatic speed – and if they do, that can often be a danger signal.

Apple's iPad and iPhones, and indeed Amazon, are clearly exceptions, but in principle most new brands take time to get established. A concern I have is that companies do not allow sufficient time to truly give the brand a chance to build a sound platform. This again is, to some degree, a by-product of the short-term bonus culture of recent years.

All brands need brand champions within the company who have the necessary tenacity (as well as support from the top) to work hard to establish the building blocks for the brands in their early lives.

Great brands develop appeal because they have something unique to offer. If they hit the spot, word of mouth – and these days social media – will get people talking about them. As and when they start to move, so advertising comes into play and reinforces the positive messages. The process should not be rushed and there is never an exact time, but if your brand is successful, there will be a dramatic upturn in demand and you will know all about it.

As a caveat, brands that grow too quickly often die quickly. Once a brand is mature, beware of the potential for decline, unless it is constantly reinvigorated.

The product life cycle illustrated by a curving graph is an old but useful tool which might help you think about your brands both new and existing.

FAME HAS MANY FATHERS

Here is another saying to ponder: "Fame has many fathers, but failure is an orphan."

My good friend Tom Jago invented Baileys, and I was proud to have been involved in driving the brand in its early years. I am astounded, however, at the number of people who claim to have invented it themselves.

I mentioned that Baileys failed in research but was launched anyway. By contrast, in the early 1980s Tom and I developed a wonderful English green cream liqueur called John Dowland's Greensleeves. It researched brilliantly and we launched it in the USA, but it was a total failure.

With hindsight, the liquid should have been brown and not chlorophyll green, but unfortunately it was too late.

I often remark that all those who claim to have invented Baileys would have trouble fitting into a football stadium, but all those who invented Dowland's would fit into a tiny telephone booth – namely Tom and me. Failure, you see, is an orphan.

CORPORATE CULTURE

Minds are like parachutes, they only function when open.
Lord Thomas Dewar, co-founder of Dewar's Whisky

I have no intention of defining corporate culture, but I do believe that great cultures involve being proud to work for a company, looking forward to going to work each day, understanding the company goals and true purpose in life and feeling that your contribution is genuinely valued. How rare is that today?

YOU KNOW YOU ARE NO LONGER CHAIRMAN
WHEN YOU SIT IN THE BACK OF THE CAR AND IT NO LONGER MOVES.

49: What sort of corporate culture is there?

Is it about status? Is it "I versus we"? Does top management really care about their key asset – their employees?

I abhor people who constantly talk about "I, I, I" as opposed to "we", the company. At the end of the day, you work for the corporation; you don't own it unless you started it yourself – and even those who do own corporations are more often likely to talk about "we" as they build their teams and their people.

Look at titles and how people treat staff. If they have chauffeurs, do they automatically sit in the back or the front of the car? Of course, if they are with someone, they should sit in the back, but if they are on their own, why not sit in the front? Think of corporate planes: are they "toys for little boys" or seriously useful and cost-effective for the business? Very rarely is the latter true.

How respectful are executives when they work with and talk to those who are lower in the pecking order? Are the latter treated as an asset or simply as someone who is paid to do a job, no questions asked? Do you think your own contribution is being valued? Or are you working in the kind of environment where your seniors effectively seem to say, 'Your idea is great. I'm glad I thought of it.'

Is the company you are seeking to join or are working for one that is truly interested in innovation? Does it welcome lateral thinking or does it prefer the status quo? If you are brought in as a "change agent", it is essential to have a champion to support you on the board, whether it is brand innovation or process innovation or whatever. Often, but not always, the older people who are nearer to retirement are less interested in change.

Essentially, innovation suggests risk-taking. The price of success requires accepting failure – not continuous failure, of course. Is there a blame culture or recognition of reality and the facts? And what can be learnt from it?

BEWARE OF COMMITTEES

Is your company a bureaucracy full of committees? These are all serious danger signals.

As the old saying goes, "I have never seen a statue dedicated to a committee."

See also: "A committee is a collection of individuals who, as individuals, do not have the capacity, ability or courage to make decisions but, as a committee, are collectively able to make a decision that no decision should be taken whatsoever." I think that speaks for itself.

It is very important to ensure that there is a genuine decision-making culture in your company, or you'll be drowned by inaction and bureaucracy.

When it comes to effective decision making, I have always believed in advisory boards with strong views but certainly not in committees. As I have heard on a number of occasions, the best committee is made up of an odd number and three is too many.

SHORT-TERM OR LONG-TERM?

Companies today tend to focus too much on short-term gains. This has been exacerbated by the bonus culture in recent years, which over-rewarded short-term profit increases. Great brands take time to build, and indeed, in the liquor industry, they can take ten years or more.

It may well be two or three years before the new brand moves into profit.

What is the attitude of top management and the board to this? If they are not prepared to take a long-term view, you will have trouble being an innovator in that organisation.

50: Don't confuse the person with the position

When you work for a company, you will almost invariably have a title that succinctly defines your role. Unfortunately, for some people their egos get in the way and, because they are promoted to a significant position with a fancy title, they think that they are very important. Suddenly, they demand all sorts of false trappings: a bigger office, a plush carpet, a better company car and, occasionally, even a company plane.

Perks and status symbols do come with the territory, but don't be confused: it is the title that has those benefits, not you the person. And, sure enough, if you were that person and lost your job, you would be Mr(s) Nobody once more.

So yes, enjoy the benefits offered as you climb the ladder, but don't think that it makes you important. I have dealt with many a pompous boss in my time, which on the one hand was mildly irritating and unnecessary, but on the other hand made me realise how insecure they probably were.

Truly great people are always modest and courteous, and know that nothing lasts forever.

A FEW COMMENTS THAT HINT AT A NEGATIVE CULTURE

Look for signals, positive and negative, which hint at the type of organisation you are working for. Here are three of my favourites:

- "Trust me."

It always surprises me when someone says, "trust me" – we should surely be able to trust our colleagues anyway, so if somebody says this to me, I am immediately suspicious.

- "I want to be honest with you."

This is even worse, and my instant reply is, "But aren't you normally?"

- "But…"

I am nervous about the word "but", especially in the context of a personal assessment. When, for example, if I'm told, "You are doing a good job, but…" I tend to think most of what comes before the "but" is bull dust.

CONCLUSION

A career is over sooner than you think, so please do thorough homework on the company you wish to join. Hopefully, you will then join a firm with a good team-building culture.

FAMILY COMPANIES

Everything must be changed in order to keep things as they are.
Frederic Rouzard, CEO of Roederer Crystal Champagne

In my career I have worked with a number of family companies. They have not all been good experiences, but they certainly have been interesting and, in the main, I have enjoyed them.

I accept that in family companies sometimes people reach the top because of their surname or because they are being protected and looked after, but today, more and more family companies are being run professionally (albeit that they may carry the odd passenger). Let me suggest a few guidelines, however, to ensure that the companies are run as efficiently as possible without undue family conflict and – more importantly – to help you in your career should you join a family company.

IN A GOOD FAMILY COMPANY THERE IS MUTUAL RESPECT BETWEEN ALL DIRECTORS – FAMILY OR OTHERWISE.

51: The essence of a good family company

What is the heart and soul of the company? One needs to be clear about the unique identity of the family company and why it is of value. Let that guide you, but make sure that at all times the company is properly run and that employees – family and nonfamily members alike – are all proud to be part of the same team.

NEPOTISM

As far as possible, nepotism should be avoided (unless strictly on merit). The days of the gifted amateur are over. However, it is sometimes inevitable, especially when the family is the controlling shareholder.

It is good to have family involved in the business, but their entry and participation ideally needs to be guided by clear criteria and ability. What is fundamental is that family executives, more than ever, should seek to earn the respect of their peers through their ability and not their name.

GOOD GOVERNANCE

All family companies today need to recognise the importance of good governance. The objective is surely to build the long-term health of the company. There should be truly independent advisors and directors, with the company using these seasoned professionals to help confirm and implement the firm's strategy. It is their independence that will allow them to challenge the strategy and also the appointment of key executives – and, on some occasions, to sanction the removal of family members, hopefully diplomatically – where they can add real value. They will also serve on the required committees, e.g. the Audit and Remuneration committees in the case of a publicly quoted company.

FAIR REWARD

Recognising that family shareholders are usually interested in dividends and the long-term future, it is vital to find a balance between motivating employees while ensuring that family members who wish to have access to regular income and dividends are taken care of.

This is a careful balancing act. I personally believe in a solid long-term dividend strategy for virtually all companies – family or otherwise. This viewpoint seems to be validated more than ever in the current economic environment.

52: Family shareholders

It's important to have good and open communication amongst the ever-extending number of family shareholders. This also creates a social opportunity for bonding and understanding of what the company is all about.

Many family shareholders are quite far removed from the business. They may not necessarily agree with what happens, but they should at least feel comfortable that the family business is well-run. If not, they will simply vote with their feet and try to exit their shares, which may be the turning point from running a family company to being acquired by someone else – especially if family ownership drops below 25% (or whatever the controlling percentage is).

Employees do not often hold shares in private companies, but if a family company becomes quoted, then bonus schemes can be implemented with advantage right down to the shop floor, including the distribution of shares in the company. In this way, a wide swathe of employees (and retired employees) can more realistically feel that they are "rowing in the same boat" as the controlling family.

It's what's known as "having skin in the game": putting your own money on the line in the business enterprise or, even as a small shareholder, having a long-term future dependant on the company success.

Many public companies, where there is no family involved, give out shares, but in these cases there isn't emotionally quite the same "boat" for the employee to get into.

53: Succession

Where possible, ensure that there is planned retirement for family members – indeed all executives, especially board members. It is good to have elder statesmen as advisers, but the enterprise must be run by the best possible people. On the other hand, elder statesmen or wise mentors can be very useful in an advisory or non-executive capacity. More than ever, especially in public companies, the best person should become the chief executive irrespective of their surname. If you need to accommodate family members, this must be carefully done through the board, as long as it ultimately achieves a positive result.

CONFLICT

Conflict is inevitable in families – or in any company for that matter. People have very different ideas and ambitions.

What one wants is a relaxed form of conflict where people compete for the best solutions via open and honest – albeit at times blunt and tough – communication. The key is to avoid getting personal. What you don't want to see is family parochialism versus executive directors. It is up to the Chairman to ensure that this does not happen.

LONG-TERM V. SHORT-TERM

Prior to the last recession, we saw a raft of companies being taken over as a result of clever financial engineering. I know of a number of cases where family businesses would have been acquired were it not for the loyalty, tenacity and long-term guardianship of the company by the family shareholders. Many of the companies acquired were simply asset-stripped or ran out of cash and have since folded.

I had the pleasure of being a director of two well-run family companies in the UK in the late 1990s and first part of this century. They are well-run by a combination of family members and farsighted employees and during my time on the board, all acquisition overtures were rightly considered but rejected. I am delighted to say that both these companies are prospering during these difficult times and will be around for many years to come.

Michael Turner, Chairman of Fuller Smith & Turner PLC, once put it to me like this:

"A family company has to uniquely look always to the long term and to the next generation. I suspect we all look at ourselves as life tenants of the business to be handed over to the next generation, and not as owners. This has enabled us to have a much more solid base and, typically, family businesses were not overborrowed when the crash came. Short-termism is the enemy of long-term growth."

CONCLUSION: PERSONAL EQUITY

It is hopefully now clear that having long-term equity in the company makes for better strategic, long-term decisions. I see this as a key to much of the worldwide growth for the big family-founded companies prospering today. The weight of family ownership varies, but the fact is that those who run the groups have a large personal stake in that enterprise.

They have got "skin in the game", a heritage that they wish to hand on to future generations and, most importantly, the decision-making is quicker and easier than in many board-managed companies and thus they are more entrepreneurial.

As an employee or hired gun, however, this type of company may not necessarily suit you and your ambition.

DOING BUSINESS INTERNATIONALLY

If you reject the food, ignore the customs, fear the religion and avoid the people, you might better stay home.
James A. Michener, author

Nowadays, many executives travel the world a great deal. But not everyone is able to transcend from a nationalistic domestic view to thinking about working with and respecting the culture of the people in different countries around the globe.

I have had to remove a number of people from international roles because of their attitude – sometimes because of their patronising arrogance towards those lower in the pecking order abroad, sometimes due to a simple lack of courtesy to others, but largely because they did not respect the people with whom they worked and who came from totally different backgrounds.

54: Multicultural adaptability

Company culture is considerably more important than is often appreciated. There is no doubt that there are vast differences between British, American, French, Chinese and Japanese cultures, and this is reflected in company culture as well. How we perceive the behaviour of others and the correct ways of doing business is very much influenced by our views of the world from our own backyard. One of the key requirements of executives working internationally is something I term "multicultural adaptability".

Too many people have an ethnocentric view of the world, operating on the premise that the ways of the home country are the best and, as such, should be accepted by others. Equally, we certainly don't want to blindly accept polycentrism, which suggests that the host country where one is doing business always knows best. What we should be focusing on as international marketers is geocentrism, which encompasses a worldwide orientation and is characterised by a positive attitude towards all people and cultures. It does not favour either the home or the host country, but tries to synthesize and transcend both ethnocentrism and polycentrism by borrowing what is best from all countries.

In other words, we cannot assume that business practices differing from those generally accepted in the United States or Europe are less relevant, outmoded or insufficient. Indeed, the converse may be the case. Marketing may initially have been developed both as a discipline and as a practice in the United States, but we now live in a global world where no one's perceptions and views have an automatic right to be considered the correct ones.

It is totally wrong to judge business in all countries by one's own domestic standards. Every country has its own unique way of conducting business affairs – whether one likes it or not.

Generally speaking, Westerners are more instant in their judgement and thought process, whereas in Asia "getting to know you and taking time in so doing" is a crucial plank to good, long-term business dealing.

Westerners often rush to first-name terms. In Asia, it is a slower process, building trust and comfort for the hopeful dealings ahead. In Japan for example, in the negotiation itself, you may find that people opposite you at the table remain silent and expressionless for quite some time. It's nothing negative; they're just waiting for you to reveal more. So don't be over-anxious to close the sale.

What these simple illustrations suggest is that you need to appreciate the psychological aspects of cross-cultural negotiations. There is no one way to do things.

Successful marketing in the world of today is geocentric in that it borrows good ideas from many countries and from firms of different nationalities. If you like, it is, or should be, a synthesis of what is best, and indeed the earlier enthusiasm about American marketing and the current fascination or concern with the Asian or Chinese ways of conducting international business illustrate this point. And let's not forget that Africa and South America are also rapidly developing continents.

After all, the world is not shrinking; it has already shrunk.

Multicultural adaptability takes time and clearly limits how fast one can grow. Being an international executive is a testing experience and not suited to everybody, so we all have to think very carefully about the attitudes and perspectives of those we wish to post abroad.

55: Appreciating different cultures

Every nation has its own way of doing business, and different cultures are influenced by various historical and religious beliefs.

This can be particularly observed in the customs surrounding the exchange of gifts – and it is worth knowing the details.

For example, in parts of Africa, if someone offers you a gift, you must always put forth both hands. This is not greed, but courtesy – to show that you have nothing to hide. In China, it is good luck to receive a gift with the number eight on it, whereas the number four is bad luck. In some parts of the world, red is good luck and in others it's bad.

When launching or building your brand, ensure the brand name is carefully tested for suitability in each language and culture in which it is to be marketed. And be very wary with slogans. Pepsi once had problems with the slogan "Come Alive", which was interpreted in Taiwan as "Pepsi-Cola will bring back your dead relatives". Some years back, Chevrolet brought out the Nova car, but they had sales problems in Europe because *"no va"* means "It does not go" in some Latin-based languages!

In China, it is also important to respect the ancient art of aesthetics and placement, or *feng shui*, which is based on practical considerations: you put a kitchen on the north side of a house because it is cooler; you sleep with your back against the mountain because it feels safer etc. You must be careful about colours too – in some cultures, for example, white or blue may be connected with funerals.

Finally, it is always important to appreciate and respect the fact that in the country you are visiting, if they address you in your language (in my case English), it may well be a foreign tongue to them, and may even be their third language. You need to be ready to interpret statements, or indeed commitments, with some degree of flexibility and tolerance and certainly with caution. For example: if you say "Yes" in Japan, it may not mean "I agree with you"; it may simply mean "I hear you".

So please, do your research about the dos and don'ts of your destination, and above all, avoid breaking local law. Trouble can be avoided by reading the relevant country's advice on the Foreign and Commonwealth Office website.

FOOD AS AN ICE-BREAKER

When it comes to food, on arriving in a new country, make a point of eating and enjoying the local food. This is a great way to build relationships and earn respect. But be aware of taboos; you may not like to eat with your hands, for example, but in India and the Arab world many people do (you must also make sure that it's your right hand).

The first time I went to Japan in the 1970s, I was taken to a French restaurant on my first night. I formally thanked my host, but asked if thereafter I could eat local food and in local restaurants. It was a great relationship breakthrough and to this day I am a lover of Japanese food.

Some years back, I was entertaining an Asian delegation in London. The leader of the party picked up his finger bowl and started drinking from it, thinking it was there for that purpose. I immediately did the same, as did my colleagues, and thus we embraced our differences and formed a bond.

These simple illustrative comments point to a general rule about conducting business abroad: seek advice from the people who live in the country you visit, and respect their culture. Not only will you build better relationships, but you will enjoy your visits much more. And remember that you will always need flexibility, perseverance, politeness and patience.

LANGUAGE

This is particularly important when you are using an interpreter, especially at meetings:

- Speak slowly and clearly and use simple words and sentences.
- Pause routinely so that listeners can take in what you are saying in their own language or ask questions.
- Emphasise key words and make eye contact with everyone – including the interpreter. In a sense you are on a stage, so you must watch your audience carefully for any reaction, as they will be watching you.
- Last but not least, if you can express a few words in the local language your effort should be appreciated.

SMILE AND LOOK POSITIVE

This simple human expression is a powerful tool in your armoury. Smile often, look interested (even if you do not understand what is being said), and others will soon respond warmly to you.

56: Business travel advice

- Beware of overconfidence, even if you are an experienced traveller. And allow for the unexpected, because yes, it does happen.
- Do have copies of your passport and useful documents not only at home, but with you when you travel. Are your key phone numbers properly backed up and not just stored on your SIM and phone memory? Will your mobile phone work on your local network or will you need a temporary SIM?
- Your family and colleagues must know your travel arrangements and contact details.
- Please ensure you have full medical cover valid in the countries you are visiting.
- Do your credit-card providers and banks know that you are travelling? More and more transactions are stopped as a security precaution.
- And last but not least, be careful at all times, especially if you're on your own and don't know the city or country well. There may be occasions when you should check in with the embassy as a safety precaution.

THANK-YOU LETTERS AND THE POWER OF FLOWERS

In my early business years, I accompanied one of my bosses to various places around the world. Whenever people helped him, he always expressed his appreciation in a tangible form. Sometimes he wrote a letter; if the secretary had done a little typing for him, he sent her flowers or some other suitable gift.

I thought this lesson really worthwhile, and as I travelled around the world, I often used to send flowers to say thank you to the women (all the secretaries were women at that time) who helped me with work that I needed done while I was away.

> I got to know the PA to a senior executive of a company I was trying to do business with in Australia. She couldn't have been more charming, and I often sent her flowers to say thank you. As a

> result of the friendship we built up, she gave me very honest but good advice about that particular company.
>
> On a subsequent trip I sat down and negotiated with her boss to try and merge our company with theirs. It was a very good merger – good for both parties – and today that company is an outstanding success in Australia. However, I do not think the deal would ever have been pulled off were it not for the information provided by that PA. It was a very tough, touch-and-go negotiation, and I was put off by the arrogance and ego of her boss – a man she did not have time for but whom she had inherited when the previous Chief Executive retired. There was nothing untoward, but what she said encouraged me to proceed and close the deal.

TIME ZONES AND TRAVEL TIPS

With rare exception, you cannot conduct international business without travelling a great deal, and this often involves crossing time zones. As a result, you will inevitably suffer from *circadian dyschronism*, or "jet lag". Your symptoms may include dizziness, thirst, memory loss, feeling hot, and wanting to sleep in meetings. You may struggle to follow what people are talking about – all very dangerous, both to you and your business.

You will not be alone in experiencing these symptoms as they affect virtually all international travellers.

The good news is that, while your body will take time to recover fully from the many time zones you have crossed (my rule of thumb is a day for two hours of time difference), there are things you can do to minimise your suffering.

DIRECTION OF TRAVEL

Firstly, going north or south makes very little difference. You may miss some sleep on the flight, but all you should experience is a little tiredness. East–west is where the damage happens, and flying east is worse.

Going west, you travel with the sun and your day lengthens. Lengthening the day is less stressful, but you will wake up earlier. Going east may well create serious problems as the day is shortened by the time-zone travel. You will have to go to sleep earlier than your body suggests, and you will wake up wanting to go straight back to bed.

UPGRADES

Travelling in comfort on the aeroplane will obviously help you to arrive in better shape. With luck, you will not have to fly economy, or "cattle class", on too many business trips. If you do, you can at least politely seek an upgrade. It is amazing how being well dressed and courteous can sometimes do the trick.

You should also build up loyalty air miles with your preferred airline which can, in turn, be used for upgrades.

TIPS TO MINIMISE JET LAG

- If heading east, try going to bed and getting up a little earlier for a few days before departure. The reverse applies to west-bound travel.
- If nothing else, be as rested as possible on the day of departure. Give yourself plenty of time to get to the plane early, settle in and relax. After checking in, take a stroll around the terminal.
- Apply a good moisturiser to keep your skin feeling fresh.
- If you can, take a flight that arrives at bedtime, local time. Eat light, especially on the plane, and minimise caffeine. Immediately after take-off, adjust your watch to the time at your destination.

COMFORT

It is always a good idea to wear loose-fitting clothes and shoes, and to use an eye mask to block out the light. Light is a crucial part of setting and resetting the body clock. If you are unable to sleep, stretch your arms and legs every few hours and take a walk if you can.

While there will always be last-minute work to do, try to put this aside for the duration of the flight. Being in good physical condition when you arrive should be your major concern – don't be a well-prepared mess at the meeting.

ALCOHOL

Although I have been in the alcohol industry all my business life, I drink alcohol very sparingly, if at all, on long flights. They say a drink in the air has the same effect as three on the ground, and the resultant hangover and headaches will not help your business dealings or the enjoyment of your foreign visit. If you must drink on the plane, do so in moderation, and whatever else, drink a lot of juice or water to fight dehydration. This also applies to the first few days at your destination.

> I learnt a painful lesson on my second visit to Japan. I arrived on a Sunday morning and proceeded to have a very long lunch with friends, accompanied by various alcoholic beverages. I got back to my hotel at 4 pm and had a short nap. That night it was impossible to sleep, and the next day, when I had important meetings, I found it very difficult and painful, as I struggled to concentrate and keep my eyes open. I have no doubt that my business discussions were negatively affected as a result.

ON ARRIVAL

When you get to your hotel, it may be tempting to have a nap. Try to avoid this, unless it is your usual bedtime. Stay up and then go to sleep at the normal local time. If possible, go to the hotel fitness centre to gently get the heart and lungs working; this will make it easier for you to fall asleep when the time comes.

If you arrive in the morning, maybe allow yourself a short nap and a brisk shower, but then find some bright light. Stay up throughout the day until local bedtime. You may sleep fitfully, but you should make good progress in readjusting to local time.

THE CONCIERGE LEVEL IN HOTELS

Most international hotels have a concierge floor, which essentially means the use of a lounge for breakfast, snacks and drinks in the evening, or simply a place to relax.

Travelling can be a lonely experience and it is good to get out of your room and enjoy such benefits. It can also be a good deal financially because the extra cost of the concierge floor is usually more than covered by the free breakfast, snacks in the evening and the drinks on the house.

If you travel a lot, it might be a good idea to be loyal to a particular hotel group. They will offer you many benefits over the course of time, including – if you earn enough points – holidays for you and your family.

SAFETY

Most travel to major countries is pretty safe, but it is advisable to keep a low profile and be discreet. There are always criminals targeting seemingly wealthy foreigners. Whatever you do, do not get into a confrontation with locals. Be polite and firm and step away. Depending on the country you visit, it may well be advisable to contact your local embassy.

SLEEP AIDS

There are mixed views about sleeping pills. I have taken them for some thirty years, but abide by strict rules: I sometimes take a mild pill on a night flight and at most for two nights thereafter, but never beyond that. And I always ensure I have some exercise, if at all possible.

PACKING

When it comes to packing, I abide by the following advice as given by Susan Heller Anderson:

"Nobody likes packing. The first agonising decision is what not to pack. The best advice is probably still this maxim: lay out all your clothes and all your money. Then, take half the clothes and twice the money."

Good luck, and enjoy your travels!

57: Go and grow where the action is

The old order has changed for ever. The initial engine for global growth was in Europe, and then the United States forged ahead and dominated the world in terms of innovation and GDP growth.

That has all changed, and in the twenty-first century the world will be much more balanced and there will be a much greater influence from Asia and Africa.

Currently, there are 7.5 billion people in the world (predicted to be 10 billion by 2050). Over 1.4 billion live in each of China and India, and both are growing rapidly. Europe has some 500 million people and economically has slowed down dramatically. America, with 360 million, is still the number one economic nation, but China is expected to catch up to, if not exceed America by 2025.

The population of Africa is growing dramatically. Although there are serious political and corruption issues on the continent, there's a lot of growth predicted. The UK has recently separated from the EU, and it will be interesting to see how a nation of 65 million people adjusts on a global basis. (As an aside, there are 2.4 billion people in the Commonwealth, now a total voluntary organisation.)

In a nutshell, far-sighted executives study the global environment and focus on the future, and look to see where economies are truly growing.

NOT EVERYONE IS SUITED TO INTERNATIONAL BUSINESS
Of course, it is not easy and if, as a business, you are going to try to develop opportunities abroad, then you have got to choose the right people to go out there. They have to be prepared to get stuck

in and not be put off by initial difficulties. You mustn't chop and change personnel, particularly in China, because it will take a number of meetings just to get through the front door.

Ideally, you should find people whose families are happy to live abroad, with all the pros and cons of such a major relocation. You simply have to be where the action is.

SHOULD YOU TAKE AN INTERNATIONAL POSTING?

Taking a posting overseas is seen by many as an important addition to their career experience and thus CV. It is essential to think very carefully and strategically about the post, however, and it is advisable to have a clear re-entry plan, lest you are forgotten while posted abroad – it can happen.

It may be exciting to accept the challenge, but ensure that your partner is in agreement. Relocation can put enormous strain on a relationship. The great adventure can turn sour unless both partners understand how radically their lives will change. If you are married, ideally you should both visit the country you are moving to in advance so you both know what to expect. Do your homework properly.

Staying put may not be an option if you work for an international organisation, and the experience you gain can have a very positive effect on your career – as long as you remember "out of sight, out of mind"; you need to work on your visibility and your network when abroad, linked back to HQ.

WHERE SHOULD YOU GO?

All international postings are a good career learning experience. There are no hard-and-fast rules, but you should ideally think about the power shift taking place across the globe. My youngest daughter, for example, has spent quite a lot of time in Africa – an interesting, challenging continent – and five years thereafter in the USA working with the United Nations. My other daughter spent four years in Hong Kong working for an international French company.

NEVER UNDERESTIMATE PERSONAL FACTORS

Family is Number One. You need to think of your partner's career, if appropriate, and where your children are in their schooling. It is also essential that your financial package should recognise and reflect your significant domestic changes on the one hand, and on the other the reality of where you are going to live.

HOW LONG SHOULD YOU BE AWAY?

Two to three years seems to be a popular cliché, but it will vary according to the country and the organisation. Transferring from the UK to the USA (and vice versa) is relatively easy, but UK to China or Japan will be more difficult because of both the language and cultural differences.

Be aware that there is always the danger of being abroad so long that you virtually become an expatriate and, for various reasons, including certain lifestyle and tax advantages, you may find yourself having great difficulty ever resettling back home.

VISITS FROM HEAD OFFICE: A HELP OR HINDRANCE?

I worry about inexperienced head office executives flying in to an overseas subsidiary for a quick visit. Of course, some bring added value, but many are often "head office seagulls": they fly over, make a lot of noise, steal your lunch, leave an unpleasant mess and then fly back home. Be wary of people from head office who simply want to have a good time and who do not show genuine interest in the work you are doing.

Conversely, if you are from head office, here is some simple advice which speaks for itself: never come back from a working trip abroad with a suntan.

FUNDAMENTAL PRINCIPLES REMAIN THE SAME

No matter where you are, the fundamental principles of good business never change:

- Good people management and cultural respect
- Good customer service
- Good marketing and overall operational excellence
- Good financial controls
- Patience and tenacity
- And at times – good luck

BUILDING YOUR BRAND

Imagination is more important than knowledge.
Albert Einstein

58: Brands have life cycles

In the Foreword, I said that everything is a brand. We as people are also brands – and have a definite life cycle.

Think of a famous footballer, such as Wayne Rooney. His active sporting cycle is short. How will he develop his brand when he's no longer playing?

What about the tennis stars, Rafael Nadal, Serena Williams and Andy Murray? What about the amazing Jamaican sprinter, Usain Bolt, who became the first man to achieve the "double double": Olympic gold for the 100 and 200m in two successive Games?

How enduring are all these brands? Do they waste their talents and their reputations? Or do they build on them in later life?

Mohammed Ali, arguably the world's greatest-ever boxer, was still an iconic brand and revered wherever he went even after he'd hung up his gloves.

People and good brand marketing influence the cars we drive, the restaurants we frequent, the sports teams we follow and, of course, the leaders we choose. You may say you are not influenced by brands, but rest assured-you certainly are. And if you don't believe me, ask your friends!

HER MAJESTY THE QUEEN

Arguably the greatest living brand of all time is Her Majesty the Queen of the United Kingdom and twenty-four other Commonwealth realms. More than one billion people watched her Diamond Jubilee celebrations in 2012. Amidst the pomp and pageantry flashed around the world was "a little old lady, dressed in the same style that she has adopted for the past six decades", as the style critic Stephen Bayley put it, writing about her brand in the *Mail on Sunday*. "Consistent, cool, uncompromising and authentic. These are attractive qualities any brand manager would kill for. Add a measure of stamina rigorously tested in global markets and you will see that if HM were a product, she would be a bestseller. Actually, she has been for over sixty years. That's not a claim Cadillac can make."

Great brands are kept in a state of constant repair. With the birth of Prince George and his siblings, the Queen has secured her brand with multiple heirs to see the monarchy through to the next century – provided, of course, that they are nurtured and guided correctly on their journeys.

THE BRAND PROMISE AND CONSISTENCY: CHANEL NO.5

For most of us, when we think about brands, we use terms like "brand identity", "brand personality", "brand positioning", etc. But the key to the great brands is timeless quality and consistency.

One of the great brands of all time is Chanel No.5. Gabrielle "Coco" Chanel set up a millinery boutique in 1909. In 1921 she launched Chanel No.5 and then in 1924 established a separate company called Parfums Chanel.

She chose a clean-cut bottle with a rectangular shape and rounded shoulders, in contrast to the ornate Art Nouveau-style bottles of the early 1900s. Amusingly, the design was said to be based on a whisky decanter used by Chanel's lover, Arthur "Boy" Capel. A classically simple black and white label complemented the functionality of the bottle, very much in line with the hats and clothes Chanel had been creating since 1909.

When she entered the export market (the USA), Chanel's bottle was strengthened slightly and given faceted edges, but fundamentally little else has changed, and it has been continuously used for over ninety years.

Distribution is carefully controlled. They stick to the simple design and endorsements by Hollywood stars. The great film icon Marilyn Monroe is famously quoted for saying, in answer to a question about what she wore to bed, "Five drops of Chanel No.5". And in 2012, Brad Pitt became the first man to be the face of Chanel No.5.

What can we learn from this experience? The No.5 design signifies "a timeless understated classic", to use a well-worn advertising phrase – an exercise in modesty and restraint, but always elegant. Simplicity is itself part of the sophistication.

Coco Chanel understood discreet seeding amongst the elite customers for her clothes and the use of enthusiastic sales assistants, building a luxury brand through carefully controlled distribution and by word of mouth. Equally important, she made a "simple" promise, which implied consistently fulfilling the expectations of consumers who are proud to be associated with Chanel No.5, with its wonderful, balanced perfume creating a fresh and lasting scent, and its consistent packaging and communication. People trust Chanel because of this promise. Chanel No.5 sells over ten million bottles worldwide every year.

The lessons of Chanel have been learnt by many others in the fashion industry. Christopher Bailey, Creative Chief Officer at

Burberry, put it this way: "I think design is not just about creation and engineering and manufacture. It's also about communication, and the environment it's going to be seen in … It's about an experience as well as buying a product."

And, of course, it's about the consistency and integrity of the promise. Can you say the same about the banking industry?

EVERYTHING IS A BRAND

Why is Coca-Cola so enduring? What led to the revitalisation of Lucozade? In the motor car industry, the Germans are enhancing and building the Rolls-Royce and Bentley brands, following their acquisition. What about the renaissance of Skoda motor cars, now owned by Volkswagen? And is Tata from India putting the fizz back into Jaguar?

Brands are omnipresent and we are influenced by them every second of the day.

Reflect on it. Believe it.

59: Creative obsolescence: the key to future success

In our accelerating world, no one can sit on their laurels. It is your responsibility to recognise the rapidly changing environment and ensure that your brands are relevant to tomorrow's world.

At times you'll have to be brutal. Coca-Cola faced reality in 1985, when they decided to replace "the real thing" with new Coke; a new formula that was supposedly better and tastier. They were wrong! Angry Coke drinkers virtually went to war with the company. Within three months, Coke's bosses capitulated and reintroduced Classic Coke.

IBM nearly disappeared and only recovered when it abandoned its focus on building hardware.

You have to constantly try something new, or paralysis will kill you. But if you get it right – and look at Apple's recovery – the world is your oyster.

MAKER'S MARK

Let me conclude by talking about a mistake a few years ago in the US which was efficiently and rapidly resolved. Maker's Mark publicly announced it was going to reduce the alcohol strength of their bourbon from 45% to 42% because they were short of stock – a seriously irresponsible statement. In other words, they were saying to consumers, "we need to make more money; we haven't got enough whiskey – therefore, we are going to reduce the strength to stretch it". This insulted consumers and there were public protests which went viral on social media. The company made a fulsome apology and retracted the announcement.

The damage was done, but at least they dealt with it quickly. We don't always get it right, but a true leader will face up to it and apologise.

60: "You" the brand

Life isn't about finding yourself. Life is about creating yourself.
George Bernard Shaw playwright

Where are you as a brand yourself? And what can you learn from the great brands of the world?

Brands are ubiquitous but need to be constantly built and refreshed. They should never be taken for granted. Likewise, you must continuously challenge your associated brands, be it the political party you support, the country you live in, the brand of car you drive, the perfume or aftershave you use and, of course, you yourself as a growing brand.

Why is Chanel such an outstanding brand? Because it is stylish and built to last. Coco Chanel herself said, 'Fashion goes, but style endures'.

Things that rise rapidly tend to die rapidly. Enduring brands will grow steadily and are constantly refreshed.

Never forget this, and think about these aspects as you shape "brand you" on your career path.

HOW MUCH TIME DO YOU HAVE?

The first twenty years of your career usually shape the direction and strength of "brand you", and the last twenty how well you commercially and financially capitalise on your own brand. At the end thereof, you'll probably have to re-invent yourself as a niche brand or elder statesman, which will hopefully serve you in good stead for the rest of your days on planet earth. After working for fifty years, I am now in the niche category, and while it may not be particularly remunerative, I find it very rewarding and lots of fun.

YOUR INTEGRITY

You may think you are a successful and wonderful person, but the truth is, your reputation is what people say about you when you leave the room. If in any doubt, I suggest you think about some of our prominent politicians.

Never do anything illegal; it is simply not worth it. There is no place to hide, so allow yourself to sleep easy, knowing that making your mark is based on your 100% integrity.

NO ONE IS INTERESTED IN YOUR PAST UNLESS IT CAN HELP THEM

Beware of the danger in boring people with your accomplishments and how good you are (it can be tempting as you get older!). Modesty is preferable, and people will find out about you anyway if they want to. Generally speaking, unless they are genuinely interested and it is a quiet one-to-one conversation, the less said the better.

So adopt the advice of only talking about your past if you think you can really help someone.

USING TECHNOLOGY TO ENHANCE YOUR BRAND

You may want to think about having your own website. If you do, it must not be an ego trip, but should succinctly reflect your background and experience, your philosophy on business and maybe life, and even some things that you have learnt that you may deem relevant. I have a simple website of my own, which I update from time to time and which I have found useful when meeting people for the first time who wish to know more about my background and commercial thinking and beliefs. A website may not suit everybody, but it is worthy of consideration.

NETWORKING AND YOUR BRAND

As you evolve your career, you are of course constantly shaping your own brand, hopefully in a positive direction. Never take your brand and status for granted. It is important to keep networking and building up a list of positive contacts who could be useful as customers in the future, or as people who can help you on the way. If you lose your job, this is essential.

So, on the basis that you never know what can happen and that it is good business practice, put positive time into networking. This may mean joining associations, attending events, accepting invitations... It is easy to sit at home because you don't feel like going out, but I always find when I make an effort, I make one or two useful contacts and meet interesting people.

Always be prepared to exchange business cards, which I suggest should be sorted, filed and periodically reviewed. It's easy to build a good digital database that one day may stand you in good stead.

61: Do you know who you really are?

Try not to become a man of success, but rather, try to become a man of value.
Albert Einstein, physicist

I would like all readers of this book to rise up the corporate ladder into senior management positions or build their own businesses and, en route, probably get married, have a family and a home with all the responsibilities that go with them. Many readers will travel a great deal and experience different cultures and countries on their journey, often leaving their loved ones behind. If you are in a very senior position, you will enjoy the benefits of travelling in style and staying in top-class hotels and having a support system to look after you wherever you are. There is no doubt that you will change because of the responsibilities you take on, the experiences and learning along the way and the benefits and perks that come with success. So as you build your career and climb the corporate ladder, every now and again it is probably a good idea to look in the mirror and decide who you really are.

A FIVE-YEAR PERSONAL AUDIT

I recommend you do an audit of yourself every five years. I suggested this at the beginning of the book when starting out, but it is equally important to repeat this exercise from time to time. We all change, and not always for the better. For some people success leads to unnecessary arrogance and pomposity.

The higher you climb, the lonelier it will get. You may have all the material benefits of success, but will you maintain the values you started out with and treat everyone with respect? You will be surprised at the number of people purporting to be close friends. The real question is: are they genuine or is it because you can be useful?

How will you treat your family, who have stood by you and will hopefully continue to stand by you, whatever road blocks cross your path?

The real message is to never forget from whence you came. Be true to the values you hopefully learnt early in your life and continue to enjoy the benefits of success, while appreciating that corporate life is shorter than you think.

Take stock of yourself from time to time and listen very carefully to the constructive comments (and possibly criticism) that you only will ever receive from close family and true friends. If you adopt this maxim, not only will it ensure you have a more gratifying business life, but when you eventually retire, the transition will be painless and enjoyable.

LEADERSHIP

You may become a leader and think you are important and have many people reporting to you; but the truth is you will only become a real leader when your colleagues truly respect you as such, because of the way you lead and motivate the team.

GOOD MANAGERS DO NOT HIDE IN THEIR OFFICES.

62: What good leaders do

So much has been written about leadership that I hesitate to add my comments on the subject, but here are a few points.

Some people fail miserably in leadership roles, even though they fare extremely well as individual contributors. Becoming a leader is about the judgement between doing it yourself and enabling a team to do it. As an individual performer you make decisions yourself; as a leader, you need to share decision-making with your team. Sadly, not all make the transition successfully.

CORPORATE CULTURE

The CEO of any organisation is the chief culture officer, and they set the tone and the way people are treated throughout the company. Sadly, too many companies deal only with physical safety and forget about health and wellbeing.

In France recently, senior executives from French Télécom received prison sentences because of people taking their lives as a result of totally unfair work pressure. I am convinced that in the UK and beyond, similar legal challenges on the grounds of lack of wellbeing and employee care are only in their infancy.

Poor mental health costs the UK economy some £40 billion per annum – £1,800 per person. Where you have a good culture, you have less sickness, less turnover, and greater productivity, so it's a win-win situation.

Let me suggest some thoughts from my experience, some of which will hopefully strike a note.

GOOD LEADERS:

- motivate people to get things done; in so doing, they invite their team to help shape the forward plans and they articulate the vision and the strategy, but in a way which gives everyone a sense of ownership. The key is inclusion, guidance and collaboration.
- see all executives positively as contributors to the future of the business.
- do not make premature judgements about people they inherit when joining a new company or taking on a new position – they carefully assess the strengths and weaknesses of their team and work to build on the strengths, while at the same time striving to minimise or even eliminate the weaknesses. Leadership is also about patience!
- foster collaboration and working together – people who give you trouble on certain days may be your best allies the next.
- use mentors and sounding boards and listen to what they say. Many people in life are lonely, and having someone to reach out to may make the difference between being motivated and successful or

ending up as a failed executive. Everyone has problems; it's how we deal with them that matters.
- always hire people who are smarter than themselves, if at all possible, and are loyal and protect the team at all times. Teamwork is the key, and a team is as strong as its weakest link. You need confidence to hire people better than yourself. Budding stars can be tough to manage, but it is far better to have the challenge of managing difficult potential stars than to surround yourself with "yes-men".
- build strong teams and respect everyone's role, no matter what it is, for everyone has a part to play as you woo the consumer with your company's offering. In a nutshell, build a strong team and remember that TEAM is an acronym for "Together Everyone Achieves More".
- recognise that at times, everyone will have personal problems of one form or another. Good leaders do what they can to help them through these. They may be strong and tough, but they also should be fair and compassionate; they have an open door for personal problems and recognise the human side of their team. So if someone's spouse or child is sick, that – to them – is their priority. They may have a very important job, but if you are a good leader, you will support them in their time of need. In some firms there are those who hide behind personal problems but, for the most part, people are hardworking and committed.
- protect the team from political nonsense. Their job is to minimise politics to enable the team to focus on the real job.
- are honest with their team and, whenever possible, will always deliver bad news in person but equally offer praise when praise is due.
- do not seek to be loved by everyone. A good leader needs to be understood and, hopefully, respected by sufficient people to get the job well done.
- do not play favourites.
- recognise that everyone makes mistakes, including themselves (but please not too often!) The only disastrous mistake is the same one made twice.

- respect the fact that almost everyone has a family and, in any event, needs to have a life outside of the office.
- accept that all leaders are criticised. They have to deal with it and accept it. What is important is to do what is right and steer the company in the right direction.

So the advice is as follows: regularly look in the mirror and calmly appraise yourself; if you are doing the right job, providing you are a team leader and work with your team, then worry not. Understanding how you are viewed by your subordinates, colleagues and superiors will positively affect your actions. Don't change or compromise who you are, but do gain insights into your strengths and weaknesses.

ARTICULATING THE STRATEGY

A good leader will also articulate the company's strategy to all the staff; no matter what some think, it isn't a secret! Employees like to feel involved and value being trusted. Tactics which arise out of strategy may at times be secret, but rarely do competitors benefit from someone leaving and passing on a useful tip. I also think it is a very good idea to entertain your suppliers and share your business thoughts with them; the better they understand you, the more they can support you.

There are few real secrets out there, and the key at the end of the day is about having great people to make the strategy work.

63: People work with you, not for you

I will repeatedly state that brands and people are the essence of good business, and indeed, everything is the brand – but it is people who make the brand.

It is people who build a nation. It is people who build a corporation. It is people who make it happen. Your job as an executive is to motivate people and, in this context, why not treat people as your most valuable asset?

That does not mean you won't have to take tough decisions. Sadly, sometimes one has to let people go, but should that happen, please ensure that you leave their dignity intact.

In my career no one worked *for* me. People worked *with* me. If you are the boss, people know you are the boss. You don't have to tell them that. You don't have to reinforce it with an egotistical attitude and talking down to people and letting them know constantly how important you are.

Instead, motivate everyone.

Let them all feel important, from the lowliest employee, right through the organisation. The rewards will be fantastic.

In summary, a company really has only two real assets – products (which become brands) and people.

64: Don't be a micro-manager

The best executive is the one who has sense enough to pick good men to do what he wants done, and self-restraint to keep from meddling with them while they do it.
Theodore Roosevelt, former US president

It is impossible to do everything in the business yourself – why else would you have a team? Therefore, it is important to have a good attitude and approach to delegating tasks. You should focus personally on the key decisions and hand down responsibility for the others, but remember, ultimately the buck ends at the top.

I believe firmly that a good leader delegates as far down the line as possible, but that it is, of course, essential to have intelligent control systems so that delegation is not an abdication of responsibility, but rather a way of getting things done effectively throughout the organisation.

Here are some key tips:

- Delegate for the right reasons and do not simply offload the tasks you don't like. Rather, delegate the tasks that are the least productive use of your own time, and pick others who may be better qualified to undertake them.
- Don't underestimate your staff, and choose the right people for the task. Core skills are important, attitude and motivation even more so. Don't just pick the person least likely to resist.
- Brief thoroughly. Delegation saves you time in the long run, but takes time to set up. Discuss the nature of the task and the challenges to be faced. Ask questions, or even request a written summary to be sure it has all sunk in.
- Worry about outputs, not methods. Be very clear about what you want to be achieved and when, but be flexible about how it is done. Encourage fresh thinking. Your people need to see that you trust them to do things their own way.
- Give them the tools that they need to do the job. You're not really delegating if you don't hand over some authority, but give too much away and things might get dangerously out of hand. I simply say: control the key variables.
- Keep an eye on how they are doing. Their performance reflects directly on yours, after all. But avoid the temptation to grab the reins back at the first sign of trouble. Doing so will harm the prospects for you both.

If at first you don't succeed, keep practising. Delegation is a skill that is well worth mastering. Do it well and you'll be admired by your team for the way you manage them and respected by your boss for what you achieve.

Alongside this must be an agreement on "no surprises". If you trust people and delegate, then it is up to them to give you early warning of problems ahead. Not only is it good sense but, at the very least, if the problems are shared with you, you may be able to find solutions and should share responsibility for the actions taken.

Delegation is motivating and helps build the decision-making leaders of the future.

> **THE ICEBERG PRINCIPLE**
>
> In the 1980s, when I was Chairman of IDV UK Ltd (now Diageo) with a staff of 4,000, the key to my management control was a double-sided sheet of paper produced once a month and discussed with my board.
>
> On that paper were the details of the progress of the top ten brands, the top ten expenses, staff numbers, debtors' days, creditors and cash flow, etc. – in other words, the key variables to have control of the business.
>
> Working on the "iceberg principle", I focused on the big numbers and only investigated in depth if there were significant variances, which allowed me to direct the business by focusing on priorities.

65: Bad news, risk-taking and failure

When there is a serious problem in the company, personnel will soon know, as the grapevine is always active. It is important therefore to be honest about bad news and deal with it openly and positively, no matter how difficult: face it, deal with it and share it.

Do also, however, prepare yourself with answers to all the questions you can identify. Invite people to share their views with you and never be personal. If there are personal issues to be dealt with, handle them in private. If you are able to provide individuals with some ownership of the problem, and together find the solution it will be good for confidence, team-building and the future.

Good leaders need to see obstacles as opportunities to try a new direction. They are resilient and are constantly seeking a route to a successful future.

Show your team that you are a leader by being calm, focused and forward-thinking. Tomorrow is another day and another opportunity.

EMBRACING FAILURE ON THE WAY TO SUCCESS

It is obvious that for any organisation to grow and develop it has to be innovative, be it in process or product, and in building brands you have to take risks.

It is stated regularly that most new brands fail, but equally one success of magnitude will make up for a string of failures. You personally will get things wrong from time to time – we all do – but it is how you deal with it that really will influence your career.

Ideally, there should be a company culture that encourages responsible risk-taking. That should not be a blame culture, but one where innovation is encouraged in a responsible manner. In IDV, we had a culture which allowed us to go out and try things. Some worked, some failed; but overall, we were well ahead.

So if failure is the price of success, you have to take risks if you are going to get anywhere.

66: Optimism v. pessimism and balance

An optimist believes that we live in the best possible world, but the pessimist fears that this might be true.

We have to deal with problems, of course, but we should equally look for the opportunity that a problem presents. Do not surround yourself with too many pessimists, for that will drag you down. We cannot all be wildly optimistic, nor should we be, but it is certainly helpful if people exhibit a positive "can-do" attitude.

Having said that, all teams need balance. A board, for example, should be positive in the round. You should, however, include at least one person who also looks at the negatives – and that is often the role of the finance director (I like to call them "Doctor No").

We learn from experience and the past, but looking positively to the future, with a sense of logical optimism, is surely the right way to go.

Personally, I believe that if a glass has 50% of the liquid remaining, it is half full, not half empty.

EXPERIENCE V. YOUTH

The 19th-century French writer Alfred de Vigny once said, "Greatness is the dream of youth realised in old age."

Truly successful companies are usually those that balance the speed, enthusiasm and drive of younger executives with the wisdom and experience (often learnt painfully) of those who have been around for a long time.

It is always a balance because you cannot buy experience, but equally, the enthusiasm of youth is a crucial ingredient for a company's future.

67: Communication is a two-way street

Too often, people talk down to their subordinates in an arrogant, one-way tone. Not only is this bad manners, but it is also very bad business practice. Everyone has thoughts and ideas, and it pays to foster and nurture talent. Why not encourage your subordinates to respond to your thoughts and ideas with their opinions? Ultimately, you may have to decide on your own, but at least (if you are a wise leader) you will have had the benefit of their input for you to digest, consider and indeed, maybe utilise.

In addition to the obvious, it also means that people feel more involved in the direction of the company, which must be good for all. But do not gain a reputation for seeking opinions and always choosing your way. This will simply stop people giving you their opinions.

68: Politics and decision-making

Companies are living political organisms and there are political troublemakers in every business.

STAMP OUT CORPORATE POLITICS

First and foremost, recognise this and then do all in your power to stamp it out by making it very clear that gossip, negative rumours and criticism of others will simply not be tolerated.

Encourage honest communication up and down the line, but actively discourage and stamp out politics wherever they exist. Otherwise, the pimple will soon become a boil.

SOUND DECISION-MAKING

All leaders are required to make decisions, or they would not be at the helm of their respective businesses. The key is to harness the talent of your people and involve them in the decision-making as far as possible. I don't mean that you should do this in a bureaucratic manner, but when you are wrestling with an issue, consult your team and seek their input. Ultimately, you will decide, but hopefully, you will have had the benefit of useful counsel. In addition, you will be helping to mould those subordinates into the leaders of tomorrow.

I have always encouraged my team to involve me if they are not sure about a certain decision. I don't want them to come to me with a problem without a recommended solution; or at the very least, I want to know why they want a decision and what they wish to achieve. We then discuss it, and when the decision is made, no matter the end result, we are in it together as part of a team.

It is important to show consistency and to support those who seek your input. So when things do go wrong, ensure that you never allow a blame culture to emerge because that is disastrous. It will generate fear, insecurity and politics, and people will be frightened to put their heads above the parapet or to seek your advice.

69: Effective meetings

There are far too many meetings in most businesses, and far too many meetings about meetings. I am staggered by the bureaucracy I have had to deal with in a number of companies.

Managers frequently convene meetings to avoid taking decisions – paradoxical, but true – and Sir Barnett Cocks once said that "meetings are cul-de-sacs down which creative ideas are often lured and then quietly strangled".

That said, meetings are a crucial part of business life, and as we climb the organisation's ladder we increasingly have the responsibility for organising and/or chairing meetings. The speed at which people share issues is very important in making faster and better decisions. So here are some guidelines:

FIRST AND FOREMOST – DO YOU NEED A MEETING?
Assuming you do, every meeting should have a clear purpose and – preferably in advance – this should be spelled out clearly, along with what you wish to achieve.

WHO NEEDS TO BE THERE?
Make sure that the relevant decisionmakers or experts are there and that "observers" are kept to a minimum.

WHEN AND WHERE?
Select the best time and location to ensure the key people are present and there is no undue conflict or other deadlines or issues. If necessary, some attendees may have to use video and/or conference calls. In an international company, consider carefully the different time zones.

THE MEETING ITSELF
If you want to be a good leader, do it properly. Do your homework, know what the meeting is all about and have a clear-cut agenda. Stick to that agenda and at the meeting itself be aware of the people you really feel comfortable with, who you can trust, and who might be somewhat awkward. If at all possible, pre-empt awkward questions, but at the same time give everyone a fair chance to express their views. There is no need for long meetings, and it's up to you, the Chair, to keep the meeting moving.

If the meeting is formal and important, have someone take minutes, but remember that you are in charge. Challenge participants if they are deviating from the stated objective of the meeting.

For good dialogue you must ensure that everyone feels comfortable. Many people will not comment, out of deference to their superior officers. I think this is a pity. There is a respectful way to do things and you should invite people to challenge constructively.

I like vigorous, challenging debate at a meeting, but if a decision is made with which you as a participant disagree, you must support the decision once you leave the meeting. Not the converse. I have seen too many people say little at meetings and then openly in the corridors denigrate the decisions made.

If you are not sure how well the meeting has gone and there are people who you can trust, ask them for their opinion, their guidance and their advice. Asking for help is a sign of a confident leader.

FOLLOW UP

No matter what actions are agreed to, there needs to be a follow-up process, as well as checks to keep things on track, be it by email, phone or face to face.

70: The Grandfather System and an open-door policy

A good company does not have an over-rigid command-and-control system. You should take an interest in people below your direct subordinates and, equally, the person reporting to your direct subordinate should be able to communicate with you on most issues. I call it "the Grandfather System".

Communication should flow in a relaxed way. Issuing instructions to people further down the organisation is not what it is about. There has to be a correct and agreed process, but communicating openly is good for morale and, ultimately, makes for better decision-making.

MY DOOR WAS ALWAYS FIGURATIVELY OPEN!

While you may be beavering away in your office and at times your door may be shut, it is important psychologically for your team to know that you are always available to them when needed.

Of course, you may be in an important meeting and not wish to be disturbed, but if someone needs to see you about a personal or business issue that they deem important, then within reason find time to meet with them and give them the benefit of your leadership and wise counsel.

A good PA, if you have one, should understand and respect the above and not be a blocking mechanism (as often happens), but rather a constructive facilitator who helps manage your diary, amongst other things, and who also ensures that those who need to see you will be able to do so.

You should not operate as an ivory tower in splendid isolation, for if you do, you will never be respected as a good leader and you will certainly not make the best decisions.

71: Being the new boss: the first 100 days

The early days in any new position are key to setting the tone for the rest of your time in the company. This is when you can make your mark and set clear goals for the future. As a leader, it is during those first few months that you will establish good relationships with your team and garner the respect you will need to be a great boss. Always keep an open mind and be wary of those trying too hard to make a good impression.

FIRST IMPRESSIONS

The people who impress you in the beginning may well continue to do so, but equally, you may find that those who are too keen to make an impression are sometimes shallow politicians trying to score points.

It may well be that the quieter person in the background is more effective. Probably the most important message I can give you is to talk to as many people as possible, to listen to everyone and to reflect before making judgements. This will also give you an opportunity to think about the company strategy. Your discussions with your direct subordinates and others should give you time to find out what they really think, as opposed to what you think they think.

We have touched upon people, but it is also good, as the new Chief Executive, to do your own mental audit on the things you notice immediately. What impression do you gain from the people who answer the telephone or from reception? Are you satisfied with the company's website (which says more about the organisation than people realise)? If customers are unhappy, how do you resolve their complaints? Is there parking for people who wish to visit your office? These are a few simple examples, but together they set the tone for your organisation.

ESTABLISHING YOURSELF

What is crucial to a leader's success in those first 100 days is a structured and focused plan other than firefighting, which will provide clear objectives and real value.

Your employees want to see and hear you, as do your key customers, suppliers, agencies, etc. Therefore, meet as many people as possible. You need to visit as many offices and factories as you can, which will give meaning to the numbers. Depending on the size of the company and its global spread, this can be a daunting task.

Meet, observe, listen, learn, digest, reflect. Then, after 100 days, consider sharing your initial findings with the people around you, so that – even if it is fundamentally your plan – all key people should have a sense of ownership.

KEEP YOUR BALANCE AND DON'T BE A BULLY

It is easy to be carried away with self-importance and the trappings of office. As the leader, and especially if you're new to the company or position, you're expected to have strong opinions, but it does not mean you are right. And because subordinates disagree or stand up to you, it does not mean they are wrong. Use your authority with a light touch. Never bully staff. They know you are the boss, so why not treat them with respect and listen to what they have to say? Don't patronise or talk down to people. Never shout, and if you have to take someone to task, do it in a calm and measured way, never in front of others. Your job is to motivate your team and get them all to give their very best for the company, and this is always more effective when they respect you as a person – and not simply because you are the boss.

POST-WORK SOCIAL MEETINGS

As the new boss I certainly do not advocate that you rush to fraternise socially with the people you work with, but, conversely, meeting periodically for a drink after work is a good way for people to relax and get to know you as a human being and not just as the boss. I have learnt a great deal in my time from these social meetings – some of it good, some bad. But more importantly, if handled correctly, this is a constructive way to build *esprit de corps*.

Don't forget, leadership is at times lonely. Sometimes those social meetings will help you as you wrestle with the challenges on your desk. Equally, they can give you an opportunity to get to know your colleagues as people working to build a great company. While you should not overtly (or even covertly) seek to find things out at a social event, it's amazing what you will learn. But remember, as it is a social scene, be respectful of what is said and how it is said.

72: All staff will watch you for leadership signals

Whenever I took charge of a division or a company, I always wrote to my colleagues setting out my expectations of them and my own commitment in return. Clearly, it was up to me to "walk the talk" and prove that my word was my bond. I would like to think that this was borne out by subsequent actions.

Here is a letter I wrote to all managers at Dallas-based Schenley USA, a company I took responsibility for while based in London, in 1988.

Dear Colleague,

The Way Ahead

'Here's what I expect from you. Here's what you can expect from me.'

Since assuming responsibility for Schenley, I have endeavoured to speak to as many of you as possible. Time is understandably a limiting factor and many of you will have a number of concerns, anxieties and general questions that you would wish to see answered.

In order to assist in this process and to set the scene, I thought I would tell you a little bit about my management philosophy, or more simply expressed, 'What I expect from you and what you can expect from me'.

Finance

Firstly, as managers of a subsidiary of a public corporation, we have to deliver for our shareholders and offer attractive opportunities for our employees. This means we must provide our shareholders with a better return on their investment than they would achieve if they had invested in comparable enterprises. It also means we have to ensure that all our employees are treated fairly and given opportunities for personal growth to match their capabilities and interests.

The financial guidelines are set by the Board in conjunction with top management worldwide. It is our responsibility in so doing to operate in a manner which is effective for the fiscal year while recognising our responsibility for the long term.

In this industry climate we have some tough mountains to climb but equally, if we work together as a team and focus our energies on the business, I believe we can get there.

Personnel

It is only by having strong, motivated and effective people that we will succeed and it is our collective responsibility to harness that talent in a co-ordinated manner for the good of the business. In this regard let me speak about the cancer of politics.

I think it is fair to say that in many companies a great deal of time and energy is spent on politics by many individuals. I absolutely abhor such unproductive activity and, should it occur, I will take the strongest measures to stamp it out immediately. Further, on a totally positive note, consider it energy that can be better directed towards building our company together.

Open Communication

I believe very strongly in encouraging open communication with all managers. We must also respond to criticism and questions in a fair, sensitive and intelligent way. I do not believe that in communicating with each other we must follow a rigid hierarchical system. This certainly does not mean that the floodgates are open to my office, but I will personally speak to as many people as possible, and equally I look forward to all the departments within the organisation working closely together, eliminating unnecessary boundaries where these could have existed before. My knowledge of the US market and Schenley in particular is considerably less than that of most of you. I welcome your constructive criticisms. All I ask is that criticisms are accompanied by positive steps suggesting the right improvements.

Clinic

During my monthly visits to the USA I will always try and make myself available to speak with anyone who believes they have some personal issues that require my attention. In effect I will try to set aside one half-day on each visit to have a semi-open clinic.

Integrity

We must never act unprofessionally or lack integrity. I am talking about how we act, not just how we talk. Perceptions are often stronger than reality. People will judge us first by what we say but more important by what we do. What we need in our organisation are actions and decisions based on logic, facts and fair play. What we do not want are shaded opinions or unfounded factors used to justify any of our actions or decisions.

No Surprises
Not all the issues required to be evaluated are always good ones. In this regard, I want absolutely no surprises. If we have a problem let us share it early and see if together we can find the solution. It is no good shutting the stable door after the horse has bolted.

Share the Glory
The future success of the company will depend on all of us together. Let us therefore not let egos get in the way of good business decisions and let us all acknowledge the contributions made by others. Human dignity and mutual respect are essential in all areas.

How to Make It Better
I believe that all of you have a number of thoughts on how we can improve the operational effectiveness of this company. This is certainly not a criticism of what has gone before but merely that all of you have your own ideas and often do not have the means to express them.

Let us ensure that we harness your ideas and hope that over the next few months you will all work constructively to present your thoughts to your colleagues for debate and challenge. I personally encourage this process and welcome all motivational suggestions that can help us meet our profit targets and improve the overall success of this company.

> **Conclusion**
>
> In conclusion I am very excited about working with you and achieving great things together. A company is only as strong as its weakest link and we must build on our strengths and eliminate our weaknesses. Let me conclude with the acronym TEAM – Together Everyone Achieves More.
>
> I very much look forward to working with you all.
>
> Sincerely,
> James Espey

73: Parting with people

A mantra of mine is "Be strong in decision-making, but kind in execution."

Decisions often affect people's livelihood, and here you must be measured and very fair. Sadly, leaders periodically have to let people go.

Take your time and think it through. Think about what is right for the company, but equally, consider those who will be affected. Sleep on it.

You have to believe in yourself and, in making decisions, it is important to do intelligent research. Ultimately, however, it is still a judgement. If it is about someone having to leave the company, treat them with respect and endeavour to leave their dignity intact.

I abhor the cowardliness and the lack of moral fibre of those who terminate people by email, phone and text. A good leader will always ensure it is done face to face and, if possible, help the person departing to face the future outside of the organisation.

If they have done something illegal, you will simply let them go and they may even be prosecuted. For most people, however, it is a shock to the system (especially if they're being made redundant due to downsizing/recession, etc.), and if your company can help them with outplacement or counselling, its reputation will be enhanced.

PEOPLE LEAVING OF THEIR OWN ACCORD

Most people leave an organisation to take up a positive opportunity elsewhere. There are, however, instances where it has to do with personnel issues and the leaver does not feel happy with the culture of the company. I suggest there should always be a constructive termination interview with everyone who leaves, so you can learn why they are going and, if it has to do with faults in the organisation, subsequently take steps to correct them.

Remember, good decision-making – and this is very much about how you handle people – can make you stronger. And, of course, never hesitate to learn from your own mistakes and those of others.

74: Joining the board

As you climb up the ladder you may, at some stage, be invited to join the board of the company you work for. If so, congratulations! But I am always amazed when I meet people who think that being appointed to the board is an end in itself – "I have made it to the top and aren't I wonderful?" Nothing could be further from the truth.

One of the first points to make is that you may be legally responsible, with all the ramifications that that entails. Yes, you have a personal view, but a board should take joint decisions, and very rarely should the Chairman have to use a casting vote.

Some people are too parochial or self-centred to be good directors. They think functionally about their division or their sector of the business only, and cannot contribute to the overall wellbeing of the organisation. If that is deemed to be the case, they should not be appointed. I remember at least two occasions in my career when I vetoed the board appointment of very senior people because of their extreme parochialism. I know to this day that they wonder why they never received an offer to sit at the top table. If they had ever considered how they interacted and contributed to the wider organisation, the answer would have been obvious. How often does one look into the mirror and face the truth? I know the decision was the right one.

75: Top Dog – the boss of a PLC

Who knows where your career will go? Some of you may even end up running a listed company. If you do, good luck – and always remember that the consumer will decide on your future and the shareholders will decide on your share price.

Never be arrogant and bear the following in mind:

1. Don't over-promise. Be comfortable with your forecasts, for shareholders will be very unhappy if you disappoint them.
2. Be honest with good or bad news. The business grapevine is very powerful.
3. Don't be personally greedy, for shareholders want to see that their interests are in line with those of the board.
4. Employ the best people – and better than you, if possible.
5. Weed out underperformers but treat them with dignity.
6. Communicate fully and truthfully in your annual and interim reports.
7. Don't overcomplicate your communications, and keep your explanations about your business simple.
8. Whatever you think, the company's performance will always be reflected in the share price.
9. Keep a close watch on the company's cash position at all times.
10. If at all possible, pay regular increasing dividends – it reassures investors for the long term, especially in uncertain times.

THE GLOBAL BOARDROOM

If you work for a multinational company, does the composition of your board and management team reflect your company's international ambitions? According to Egon Zehnder, the global executive search company: "In the US, companies where foreign nationals represent a third or more of the board outperform the rest of the big 500 quoted companies."

Many companies, however, are still too loaded with people "too much like me". This is surely a waste in our global village, and – providing there is a strong, well-balanced chairman – I believe the broader the constituency of the company (reflecting market reality), the better the results will be. Make sure you also address the gender balance positively.

OTHER THINGS TO CONSIDER

The smallest deed is better than the greatest intention.
John Burroughs, conservationist

BEWARE OF COMMUNICATION OVERLOAD.

76: What really matters?

It is always better to be effective rather than efficient, although both have a place. Effective means you get a result; efficient – not necessarily. It may look pretty, but sometimes, what does that matter? Has it helped the business? For example, you can spend all day trying to find the missing 5¢ in balancing your books. That may be mandatory for tax purposes, but it is certainly not effective in growing the business. You can repeatedly dig a hole in the road and fill it up efficiently, but what does it mean?

In business, as Jessie Potter once said, "If you always do what you've always done, you'll always get what you've always got."

GARBAGE AND INFORMATION OVERLOAD

Far too many people think the more data they collect and the more they write, the better they will be perceived. Wrong!

Garbage in, garbage out!

I firmly believe great ideas should be written down on one sheet of paper and presented as such. I fully accept that information technology plays a critical role in business life – accelerated by cloud computing – but today we are flooded with data.

While IT is critical, and has changed the way we do business, it shouldn't become an end in itself. Yes, organisations must and will have Chief Technology Officers and the like; but we must never lose sight of the fact that the ultimate purpose must be to do a more effective job in the marketplace.

> I remember some thirty years ago, in my Seagram days, the Chief IT officer telling me how proud he was of his $100 million IT budget. The problem was he didn't understand that the company's real job was to offer brands that the consumer wanted and that IT was a means to an end and not an end in itself. Interestingly enough, shortly thereafter, a number of expensive new systems were introduced, which had no real purpose and were a waste of money. Think about your own company!

WHAT IS SAID V. WHAT IS MEANT – FUN, BUT OFTEN TRUE

"We could certainly look at that"	"Not now, if ever"
"Frank and open discussion"	"Major row"
"I entirely agree with you, but …"	"I totally disagree"
"Let me make a suggestion."	"This is what I've decided"
"Ambitious"	"Ruthless"
"This is the last chance to buy …"	"…Until the next deal"
"You are doing well but …"	"You are in trouble"
"We must have a meeting"	"I am not really interested"
"Performance counselling"	"A dressing down"
"We have a golden opportunity"	"We are in a mess"
"Urgency"	"Panic"
"Filed"	"Lost"
"Deficit"	"Significant loss"
"This scheme has worked well in the past"	"We have run out of ideas"
"The target is a bit hopeful"	"It's bloody ridiculous"
"It's too early to see how the brands are doing"	"I think we have failed"
"Advertising investment is up compared to last year"	"We haven't got around to cutting it yet"
"Adverse consumer reaction"	"The boss's wife did not like it"
"Fringe benefit"	"Theft"

77: The use and abuse of consultants

There clearly is an important role for consultants or there wouldn't be so many successful consulting companies around. I am always surprised, however, when companies with a problem rush to bring in consultants at great expense. If you are to use consultants, you must know exactly what problem you are trying to solve and why you believe you cannot solve it yourself.

It is often said that consultants borrow your watch and charge you for the time. In the beginning they gather an enormous amount of data and ask many questions, which they usually return to you in a very attractively bound, expensive and heavy dossier. Sometimes they do superb work – but be very wary before you rush to sign them up.

Far too often, companies neglect the great talent within their own organisation, which is their own team. In the first instance, why not involve junior and middle management in looking at the issue and seeing what solutions they can find? You may be amazed at what is unearthed, both in terms of potential solutions and future managerial talent.

In the 1980s, when I was involved with a major change project in the UK, I introduced an internal Action Learning MBA programme connected to a business school, which combined academic learning with dealing with real-life business experiences. Many of the action learning projects were extremely well done and certainly a lot less expensive than bringing in external consultants. A number of the MBA graduates moved on to significant positions both within and outside the company.

Conversely, I went through a very negative experience some twenty years ago when I was a non-executive director of an own-label foods company, which was struggling and had serious cash-flow problems.

The Chairman decided unilaterally to call in consultants who, at a board meeting, promised the world in terms of potential savings; but of course, a high fee was required en route to the "promised land". I opposed the appointment and suggested that, if we were to use them, we should pay them a small fee upfront, but a significant amount at the end, as a percentage of the savings generated. This was rejected, and it was no surprise to me when, six months later, the company was considerably out of pocket, but more importantly, now had even more serious cash-flow problems.

> We had trouble keeping our lenders at bay and eventually I had to fire the Chairman and close the company, which was not a pleasant experience at all. To this day I believe the company could have been saved if the high payment to the spurious consultants had not been made and we had better harnessed our internal talent.
>
> Let me be clear, I am not opposed to consultants and have worked with some great ones, but you should fully understand what you wish to achieve, what the cost will be and what outcomes you expect. Make sure that they are working for and with you, as opposed to telling you what to do. You must be in charge, and must accept the ultimate responsibility.
>
> Consultants can be extremely valuable in a merger or acquisition situation, which I'll briefly discuss in the next section.

78: Mergers and acquisitions

A merger is sometimes like blending a philharmonic orchestra with a jazz band – together they make a horrible sound.

Buying a company or merging with another to achieve synergy benefits is great in theory, but sadly in a number of cases the weakness lies in the post-acquisition/merger process. A successful acquirer needs positive competences and strong processes to manage the merging of two organisational structures, while retaining and motivating key employees.

So before you rush off and buy a company, reflect carefully on your integration capability.

Who is who in the zoo? You need to decide fairly early – and don't just be impressed with the people making the best speeches in the company taken over. Do not hesitate to learn from the experience of others.

Ultimately, it is about effectively bringing systems, processes and people together. People are, to me, always the most important because naturally they are the keys to a successful merger and, over time, the establishment of an integrated culture.

> ### LESSONS FROM THE GUINNESS EXPERIENCE
>
> I joined United Distillers in 1986, shortly after the Distillers Company Limited was acquired by Guinness PLC (now Diageo).
>
> Ernest Saunders, the Chief Executive of Guinness, relied very heavily on a management consulting firm, and many millions were paid for their services. They did a great deal of good work, but I believe there was also much waste and there were far too many unnecessary mistakes. In many instances, the consultants acted as if they were running the company. This was clearly an Achilles' heel in Saunders' armoury, and this weakness was eventually exposed, with serious consequences.
>
> Shortly after the takeover, Saunders made a patronising speech in which he said that everyone in Distillers Company Ltd (DCL), the acquired company, was useless. What a dreadful, demotivating address! While much of top management left a lot to be desired, there was a great deal of talent beneath the top layer, and our job after Saunders' bad start was to harness that talent and motivate the team. We did our best to recover the situation and, in fairness, in many cases made good use of the Bain consultants working with us. One of the problems we were dealing with was egos, both with Bain and very senior Guinness executives.

Sadly, many takeovers fail because of the egos at the top of the acquiring company and also a lack of true financial due diligence to find the nuggets, in order for one and one to end up making three.

In the case of the Distillers Company acquisition by Guinness (see the preceding box), it was simply a badly run set of fiefdoms, operating a wide range of brands as if they were competitors. It did not take much to pull it all together and build a great company, which, of course, is half of the very successful Diageo today.

MY CANADIAN EXPERIENCE: CHOOSING THE RIGHT PERSON FOR THE JOB

During my time with United Distillers, I was responsible for our Canadian operation. We acquired Schenley Canada in the late 1980s. After the acquisition, we reviewed the directorate at both companies and came to the conclusion that the Chief Executive of the acquired company was clearly the better man, and so appointed him as overall CEO. We then looked through both companies – objectively and dispassionately – to fill all the appropriate appointments.

Obviously, the CEO of Distillers Canada was extremely disappointed, but we treated him with professionalism and dignity and he retired early with an attractive pension. We kept in touch for many years and he personally acknowledged that we had made the right decision.

As I say, be strong in decision-making, but kind in execution.

79: Clarifying leadership and communication

WHO IS IN CHARGE OF COMMUNICATION?

Ultimately, responsibility rests with the senior person in the company, but all management has a role to play in internal communications, whether it is a directive from the board, a marketing or sales initiative, or an HR message.

Start by acknowledging that all messages are open to misinterpretation. It is important to craft them as professionally as possible because bad messages, like careless talk, cause problems.

It is also wise to involve and gain the support of line managers, who often have to interpret the messages face to face with their teams, so at the very least they must know what is expected of them.

CONSISTENCY AND TRUTH

Think very carefully about the message and its objective. It must be credible and have a clear purpose. I am both bemused and saddened by corporate messages and philosophies from the top which are never practised by those issuing them.

Don't try and pull the wool over your team's eyes: they are almost invariably brighter than you think. Many managers frequently assume that because people are below them, they will believe and accept whatever has been said. This is absolute nonsense. Always treat your subordinates with respect with all communication, for truth will always emerge, sooner or later.

LIVE THE BRAND

As stated often, everything is a brand – be it you, the company or the products you sell. The stronger your brand and the more authentic, the better all will be. It is people that build brands and companies, and therefore what you say to your people should be consistent with your organisation's brand values and with what you tell the outside world.

COMMUNICATION OVERLOAD

In an electronic world it is very easy to send out too many messages. Overloading people with communications can lead to the real message not getting through. Sometimes less is more. And when sending out emails, please don't CC anyone unless it is necessary.

MARKET YOUR MESSAGES

We all like to be entertained. While our business has a very serious purpose, why not learn from marketing, and dress messages and stories in an interesting way to get the message across. It need not always be a boring email or notice on a board.

RESULTS

Periodically you should measure the success of your communication efforts. A message for a message's sake has no purpose. What did you want to achieve and how effective were you? Most people are very busy; never forget that they are bombarded with messages and communication from many different sources. Messages have to hit the mark: monitor your success.

80: The good and bad of economic fluctuations

We have had a long bull run post the 2008 crisis, so for many of you, recessions will be a far-off memory, or even unknown. On the other hand, recessions have been with us since the market economy took root and during anyone's life they may come and go with varying degrees of severity.

Possibly, the difference this time is that electronic media make global rumours and gyrations instant. And of course, we are living in a global village, with dynamic growth in China, India and elsewhere.

While economic problems cause pain, it is also a good time to bring economies and societies into balance. In more recent years, we have seen too much avaricious behaviour from too many fast deals and excesses, especially in the financial world.

What society needs is genuine, sustained brand building, putting real value into perspective, and eliminating shallowness with the much-abused word "respect". While painful, it is essential to see downturns also in a positive light.

CORPORATE WEEDING

During downturns, efficient companies weed out weak staff, trim fat, focus on cash and prepare for the good times that will always re-emerge. "Faint heart never won fair lady" – preparing for the future should be the name of the game.

Equally, while you are doing all you can to trim the fat and restructure the company during a downturn, you cannot shrink your way to greatness. If you start slashing your marketing budget, you might get away with it for a while, but eventually you will start to distance yourself from the real boss, the consumer. You may have to be more creative about how you spend your money, but please ensure that there is a consistent message with the marketplace and you also have enough good people to help you sell to your customers en route to the consumer. Under all circumstances, it is about an affordable but vital long-term perspective while recognising the environment.

WHAT DO GOOD LEADERS DO WHEN TIMES ARE HARD?

Good leaders act quickly, firmly and fearlessly. That means facing bad news head on and being truthful about the problems of the business. People can always sense evasion. You may be nervous yourself, but you have to show strength, leadership and decisiveness.

As Giorgio Armani said, opening his Manhattan store in the middle of the 2009 recession (estimated cost US$40 million), "An entrepreneur shows his true colours in a period of crisis, not in a period when everybody is having a success."

While it should be normal practice, leaders more rigorously evaluate employees during a downturn to find the stars and to weed out the weak. Employees, in turn, need to take evaluations very seriously, if they are serious about their future.

Good leaders re-evaluate the goals for the company and focus less on stock-market performance and short-term bonuses (thank goodness) than on earning a good return on the company's assets and planning for tomorrow.

A stock market decline is a good time for true risk analysis, especially those risks that have been swept under the carpet. More than ever, companies have to focus on cash generation and the risk inherent in the strategic decisions taken.

A wise company will tap the gold mine called "staff". People are the most important assets of an organisation, and everyone from the top to the bottom should be encouraged to contribute with ideas. It is amazing how effective this can be.

Tough times are also a great opportunity to renegotiate costs such as energy, telecoms, transport, etc. Clearly, it is also a good time to negotiate construction work, if you are able to finance it. A lower cost base prepares you positively for the future.

A wise leader prepares for the upturn. Downturns are bruising experiences, but they always end, and it is important to have good communication at all times with your employees because how people are treated is vital when it comes to preparing for the upturn. Rest assured that a culture with good communications and trust is one well placed to take advantage when the sun shines again.

HOW DOES THIS AFFECT ME?

Yesterday is not ours to recover, but tomorrow is ours to win or lose.
Lyndon B. Johnson, former US president

This is your concern, of course. I truly believe that far too many people made too much money too quickly in recent years without realising why. Young people thought it was easy to rise up the corporate ladder. The financial world had a magnet and a charm of its own.

I want society to focus on real, sound brand-building, where businesses grow because they deliver genuine value to the consumer; and you, as an upwardly mobile executive, will participate in steady, solid growth, creating a dependable, long-term future for you and your family.

PLAN AHEAD
This is an opportunity to stand out from the crowd. Think about your career development rather than promotion. If you have a routine job, seek to do something different – for we all need to be

re-energised. It is up to you, especially during your appraisals, to suggest how you can grow your job to the benefit of your employer and thus yourself. Be sure, however, in so doing, that you are adding real value to the organisation in the first place.

It is your responsibility to ensure that the company sees you as an asset, and thus a brand with prospects. When times are tough, and lots people out of work, this is more important than ever.

CHANGING JOBS

A business relationship without a future is like sitting in a car without wheels. You can stay in it all you want, but it isn't going anywhere.
Anonymous

IT'S NOT SO BAD BEING FIRED.

Nowadays, people change jobs and move to other companies several times in their career, and good luck if you are on the way up! But be very careful before making a decision to move. Think it through fully and talk to your close family. Do not be impetuous in making your decision.

Here are a few clues – positive and negative – as to why you might consider moving (there are many others):

- You see good opportunities elsewhere and no real progress in the company employing you.
- You are not learning and thus not progressing.
- Your opinion seems not to be valued.
- You do not look forward to coming to work – especially after a weekend.
- You are no longer proud of the company you work for.

81: Be a good leaver

I am always saddened when I hear of someone I know running down their company as they are about to leave.

You may have had a bad experience, and I have been there myself, but be very careful about knocking the company. Find a good explanation to graciously inform outsiders the reason for your exit.

Speak well of the firm and the people within it. There have been a number of instances when a bad leaver, who ran down their firm, moved elsewhere only to find the new firm acquired a year or so later by the very company they had left.

It is also worth noting that companies and people do change and you could even be headhunted back to your old company. Lastly, it is good old-fashioned manners and courtesy anyway.

PLAN YOUR RESIGNATION CAREFULLY

Like most people, I have worked for a number of companies, and I have done my best not to burn bridges upon leaving. and on leaving to move on, I have done my best not to burn bridges. My mantra has been, "If at all possible, leave in a way that could allow you to return." You may be unhappy where you are, you may be excited about the new job, but do not gloat. Rather, be gracious and show appreciation for the time you have spent with the company.

Put your resignation in writing; this confirms your seriousness. If you have an exit interview, be measured, calm and constructive. Last but not least, if you do receive a counter-offer to stay, ask yourself: is it simply a bribe to keep you a little longer, or a genuine wish not to lose you?

A FEW TIPS TO REMEMBER

You may want to share your negative thoughts, but do not – because they will soon get out. Talk to your family and trusted friends, maybe, but not to your colleagues. And if you really must, at least wait until you have formally resigned.

Act like a true professional and prepare a proper handover, ensuring that all loose ends are tied up and the transition is as smooth as possible. Make sure your clients know about it, but only in a positive way.

Ask for a reference because – unless your time with the company has been most unsuccessful – it may stand you in good stead and in any event may well be requested.

82: The grass isn't always greener on the other side of the fence

This old adage is very true.

Remember, companies that woo you always put their best foot forward. They very rarely tell you the bad things about the firm, for fear that you will not accept their job offer.

In reality, all firms have their internal issues. Before you desert one company for another, do as much homework as possible to find out about the type of culture operating in the new organisation.

I personally learnt the hard way. In one career move, I was so excited by the challenge that I didn't do enough homework to appreciate the negative issues that made it difficult to operate in a truly effective and enjoyable manner.

So think carefully before you move, and remember, sometimes the devil you know may be the best option.

DON'T RESIGN WITHOUT A FIRM WRITTEN CONTRACT

I often hear stories about people resigning from their existing jobs on a verbal promise to go elsewhere, only to have their hopes dashed to the ground.

We are often pawns in the game and companies don't always respect their greatest asset – which is the people working for them. I have known cases where three different people were offered the same job, for which only one position was available. This is totally immoral, but it happens from time to time.

So before handing in your notice to go to pastures new, wait for a firm written contract which conforms to your expectations, and do not resign until you are 100% satisfied. As explained in Tip 8: when negotiating terms with a new company, build your exit strategy in before the wedding, let alone the honeymoon because, sadly, good things do often come to an end. Sometimes in this ruthless world, the firm simply decides to dispose of your services.

83: Getting fired is not always bad!

In November 1997, when I was the Chairman of Chivas Brothers and thought I was doing a great job, I got fired. It certainly was a shock to me and my system and, equally, a wakeup call. Ironically, the catalyst, the Chivas Regal 18 brand that I launched against the Chairman's wishes, is a great success today.

Many people are made redundant or lose their jobs. Sometimes this may be fair, sometimes grossly unfair. Should it happen to you, once you are over the initial shock, you must take positive steps to move forward in your career; keep the period of feeling sorry for yourself as brief as possible. Look in the mirror, do a SWOT analysis (see Tip 2), and take good stock of yourself.

Complaining about what has happened will not feed your family.

WHAT ARE YOU ENTITLED TO?

I would like to think that there is a proper consultation process in your company, with a reasonable notice period or paid leave if you have worked there for a couple of years or more.

I would hope that you had a proper contract when you joined the company. Each country will have its own employment laws and you might be wise to take legal advice.

Whatever, ensure you get all you are entitled to.

WORKING OUT YOUR NOTICE

If your company gives you a decent notice period, this would be a good time to be proactive.

For a start, update your CV and ask your friends and family to be brutal about it. You should immediately start applying for positions – and a decent employer should give you time off to search for jobs and attend interviews.

Some companies offer career-transition services to employees who are made redundant, and of course, in this era of technology, you should also use the internet and the various jobs websites.

UPDATE AND BUILD ON YOUR NETWORK

We are social animals and networking is a part of life. It is important in business and vital if you are suddenly on your own. It is a good way to share problems and experiences, and learn from others.

So here are a few tips:

1 Build up a good database; it should have some information about the persons concerned, possibly including birth dates and anniversary dates, etc. People like to be remembered.
2 Immediately have your own business card printed, and when networking, do not hesitate to ask people for theirs. Often it is wise to follow up without seeking anything in return. You never know what the future holds.
3 While there are times when you may not feel like it, attend networking opportunities, e.g. conferences and business gatherings. After all, if you don't put a line in the water, you will never catch a fish.
4 Treat people with respect and don't just walk away because you think someone else might be more interesting. A stranger is just a friend you do not know.
5 If you are seeking a new job, appreciate that most jobs are not advertised, so you should think creatively about how you can use

your professional and personal contacts – and don't hesitate to use online social networking tools such as LinkedIn and Twitter, etc.

IT IS NORMAL TO FEEL EMOTIONAL

Redundancy sometimes marks the start of a depression, which may have been lurking for some time. Many people experience this and there is nothing to be ashamed of.

The brain is a circuit board, which from time to time may have to be rebooted. So be it. But seek help and also ensure that you use this time to get yourself into physical shape – far too few people look after their bodies, which in turn helps look after their minds.

HOW WILL YOU COPE FINANCIALLY?

This is clearly a major problem and one that must be faced truthfully and honestly.

You may have to make some significant changes to your lifestyle – but it should not really matter. The reality is that your family, your friends, your health and *enough* money are all that matters. True friends judge you as a person, not by the clothes you wear and the car you drive. So appraise your circumstances and do all you can to balance your books.

CHANGE DIRECTION?

This may be the ideal time to change direction. Could this be an opportunity to pursue the career you have always wanted – one that could potentially be more fulfilling? Is money your god? Or do you feel contributing to society (e.g. teaching or working in the charity sector) for less pay could be more rewarding in itself?

You may wish to use your redundancy to retrain, or even to start your own business. Open your mind to all opportunities and think laterally.

INTERIM WORK

Please do not be too proud to take interim work, no matter what, to pay the bills. Sometimes this leads to opportunities you may never have thought existed. The important thing is not to let your ego control your actions.

A friend of mine who ran a successful public-relations company and then got into financial trouble through expanding too quickly, ended up driving a taxi. He was at peace with himself and content with his life and his true friends, who never deserted him. Too many people are preoccupied with their status in the eyes of others. In truth, it is irrelevant as long as you and your family are happy.

WORKING FROM HOME

Working from home is becoming more and more common and many people thrive on it. If you lose your job, it may be necessary – at least for a while – and, providing you are able to adapt, it can be very rewarding.

Although some people relish being at home, others miss the social element of the office. But if you have a young family, it is a very useful option, for your children grow up faster than you think. If you retire or are made redundant, working from home can be a blessing and is usually a necessity if you wish to stay active.

TIME FOR A BREAK?

If you are in the fortunate position of having enough money, you may even feel it worthwhile taking a sabbatical – a temporary break from your career – and doing something different.

You may decide to climb one of the great mountains of the world. You may decide to work in your local community, helping people or simply to raise money for a deserving charity. This can be very cathartic and often leads to career-changing benefits.

However, don't leave it too long to get back on your business feet, if that's what you want to do. The corporate world has a short memory.

CONCLUSION

So losing your job is not the end of the world. It happened to me over twenty years ago and I am delighted with the way my career changed.

Life is an interesting journey. Enjoy it.

STARTING YOUR OWN BUSINESS

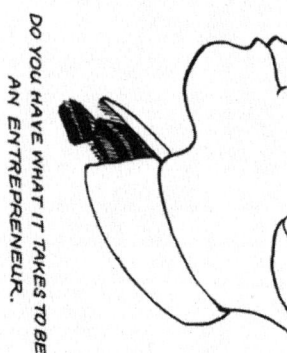

DO YOU HAVE WHAT IT TAKES TO BE AN ENTREPRENEUR.

84: Why are you starting a business?

Just because you are a good cook does not mean you should open a restaurant. You have to ask yourself questions such as: am I able to offer true value and a great experience to my potential customers? What is my unique selling proposition? In the beginning when I am an unknown start-up, will I have enough cash to stay alive? As I grow, will I be able to finance growth?

Working capital requirements are inevitably more than you think and usually the greatest cost is staff.

What is it about the offering that is so unique and special, that people will consistently wish to repeat purchase? Selling something once is not building a customer base. Remember, repeat customers are the key to establishing a brand.

To be really successful you must help solve people's problems or provide them with opportunities they did not know existed. Akio Morita, of Sony fame, noticed workers with Boom Boxes on their shoulders. He realised that what they wanted was music "to go" and this led to the introduction of the Walkman. Of course, this was superseded by the iPod, and now we do not carry separate devices at all; we can stream music directly on our smartphones.

Please also appreciate that one in five new businesses shut in the first year, and more than half go under.

KNOW YOUR DEFINITION OF SUCCESS

People will have different definitions of success. Only by knowing what you understand by "success" can you benchmark your progress. Most successful companies are based on long-term views and not quick profits.

YOU MUST HAVE REAL FOCUS AND COMMITMENT

This is hugely important, but it can be difficult to achieve, particularly for tiny start-up companies. Keep on track – too many get distracted by small difficulties. Only when you know your roadmap can you correct your journey.

Too many people will try to keep their old job on while starting a new business "in case it fails" and are half-hearted in their new venture. They have failed before they start. There are many exceptions, but never underestimate the magnitude of the commitment required by your new business.

85: Finding the perfect partner

Not every entrepreneur starts on their own, and many of the great companies began as partnerships – just think of Proctor & Gamble, Marks & Spencer, etc.

There is no such thing as a perfect partner, but if you are to have a partner, make sure they are complementary and share your ethos and mission. Be very clear what you want from them and remember that there should be a balance between the real entrepreneur/risk-taker and others who may exercise a degree of caution.

Fundamentally, you have to determine if being in a business relationship with that person makes business sense: are they a friend first, or someone to be in business with first? Problems often arise with friends going into business when one can't hold the other accountable to their job for whatever reason. You may be friends, but can/should you be business partners?

WHAT HAPPENS WHEN BUSINESS RELATIONSHIPS TURN SOUR?

You must be courageous and confront the situation diplomatically. Ask questions, understand the position and listen carefully. If it is a one-off problem, ask what needs to happen to avoid a recurrence and remember to focus on the issues without being unduly personal. If it doesn't work out, it is better to deal with it sooner rather than later for the business' sake and, of course, for the individuals.

86: Raising money for a start-up

There is no magic formula and it is usually a case of tapping all your resources, including family and friends. It is important to be brutally honest about the risks and the possibility of failure.

The time to buy an umbrella is when it is not raining. Likewise, the time to get an overdraft from the bank is when you don't need one. I have kept an overdraft facility with my bank for thirty years on a "just-in-case" basis.

Oscar Wilde once said to always borrow money from a pessimist, because at least you know they won't expect it back. But in a serious vein, you may have to mortgage your house, sell your car or other valued possessions. This requires a passionate belief in what you are doing, coupled with tenacity and the determination to sail through stormy seas, for that is an inevitable part of a new business.

You will also need to keep costs to a minimum when starting out. Avoid fixed costs if at all possible. Perhaps work from home and use coffee shops and libraries that offer free Wi-Fi and a plug socket. Another tip is to hire a meeting room by the hour, and staff by the day and only as needed.

87: The hockey-stick rule

Whatever plans and projections you have, there is no such thing as a straight-line forecast. Your expenses may be consistent (if only consistently more than you thought), whereas your sales and profit line usually go below budget before, with a bit of luck, taking off like the shape of a hockey stick.

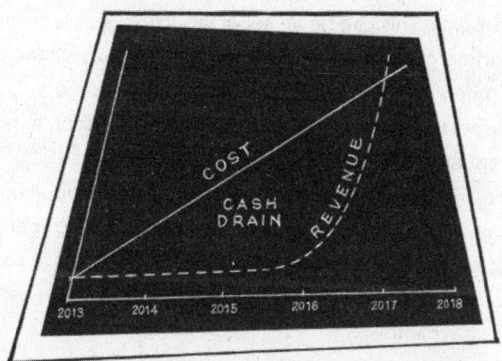

It usually takes twice as long and twice as much money as you ever thought to break even – can you last the journey?

Most new companies take quite some time to get established and many die because they run out of cash.

88: Managing growth

Far too many entrepreneurs have great ideas without any understanding of how to convert them into a profit – which essentially means managing growth and ensuring a positive cash flow.

Here are some tips to help you:

1. Seek advice: find a business mentor who has been there. Learn from others' mistakes and benefit from their hard-earned wisdom.
2. Know as much as possible about your customers before you start trading with them.
3. Build a careful relationship with your chosen bank which must always believe you are in control of your business.
4. Do you fully understand what a positive cash flow means? If not, you'll soon be out of business.
5. You have to balance your creditors and your debtors. Creditors/suppliers can be very demanding and debtors are often late with their payments. This can be an especially large problem when you are importing goods from another country because of the time lag from shipment to arrival and the sale to your customers.
6. Lease assets to cut commitments. Leasing is, in effect, a rental agreement and is generally a tax-deductible expense.
7. Have constructive strategic discussions with your suppliers.
8. Be as lean as possible with your stock holding. Remember JIT (Just In Time): a number of companies die because they have too much stock (cash negative) and therefore too long a time lag between sales and payment.
9. If need be, you may have to liquidate stock quickly and creatively.
10. Beware of over-trading. It may seem exciting to have rapid growth, but – simply stated – if more cash is going out of the business than coming in, you are in trouble. Sufficient working capital to finance growth is crucial.
11. Within reason, everyone within the company should be involved in managing cash, but of course, you must be constructive and

positive in how you deal both internally and externally with the cash situation and consequent health of your business.

12 A cash-positive business with slower-managed growth will ensure a long-term future. As you know, you can't bank turnover and profit: you can only bank cash. You need to think very carefully about how you husband your cash. For further tips, see Tip 32 on how to manage cash flow.

CREDIT MANAGEMENT

Economic uncertainty and the breakdown of the banking system has badly affected global credit for many. This has brought into focus the importance of effective credit management.

Beware:

- Customers often take longer to pay than agreed – and the big boys are sometimes the worst. Worse still, if a customer goes bankrupt, you never get paid!
- Debts must be managed very carefully, or bad debts will soon arise.

It is essential, therefore, to know who your customers are if you give them credit, and to agree clear payment terms before supply. Consider discounts for payment with order and also factoring as an option. Invoice promptly and do not be afraid to ask for payments.

Good credit-control departments watch out for danger signals, which are essentially changes in practice from customers. They may include some of the following:

- An increase in complaints and dealing with staff you do not know.
- Difficulty in contacting people, and calls being blocked by unhelpful staff.
- Customers starting to settle late.
- Customers changing banks.
- Customers refusing to pay anything because of a dispute over a tiny amount.

Let me quote from Peter Drucker, renowned author, professor and management consultant: "The most important thing in communication is hearing what isn't said."

So be wary of negative body language, lack of eye contact and general signals of discomfort. Non-verbal communication often says a lot more than people realise.

PREDATORS

When you are desperate, predators and the venture capital world will happily take control of your business for a song and then where do you stand? At best, you'll end up being a tiny shareholder and at worst, an employee – or even elbowed out.

CREDIT CARDS: THE LAST RESORT

Here is a final – and unusual – tip: when you start your business, take out every single credit card you possibly can, but do not use them. Put them in a safe place and use them only as the ultimate last resort and providing you truly believe your new company/brand has a future and simply needs to weather the storm. Then, and only then, should you draw on those credit cards.

BUILDING A NON-EXECUTIVE CAREER

89: Where to start

Ideally, you should start planning your non-executive career when you are in full-time employment and, hopefully, building a good reputation. A non-executive appointment with an entirely different company can also be good experience which may help you in your own business.

I spent most of my career in the liquor business, but my first non-executive appointment was as a Director of Church Shoes PLC, while I was the chairman of Chivas Brothers.

A few simple points:

- Keep your CV in a state of constant repair and shape it accordingly.
- If you have an executive job, make sure your superiors are happy for you to take an outside appointment.

- Quietly start networking and letting people know that you are interested in becoming a non-executive director, ensuring that you are clear about what you can contribute.
- Most search companies have a non-executive division and you should make a point of arranging to meet the appropriate people in those companies so that they are aware of your intention. Non-executive appointments often arise when you're not expecting them!

90: Key role of a non-executive director

First and foremost, you are now a helicopter pilot and not a micro-manager. The helicopter must fly and land safely, but you are not expected to understand every detail of how the gyration system works or how it is constructed.

On the other hand, as a non-executive director you must ensure that the right top management team is in place, the company operates at all times with fiscal probity, cash management is omnipresent and there is a sound strategy and execution plan.

In one of the companies I joined, my fellow non-executive director, who was in charge of the audit committee, was a micro-manager who thought he was the finance director, and we spent many unnecessary hours in meetings about minutiae. He did not last long.

YOUR FIRST 100 DAYS: ASK, LISTEN AND LEARN

The first 100 days are the foundation that will help you to be a more effective non-executive director; Spend as much time as you can using shoe leather by visiting plants and offices and listening to people telling you about how the business operates. Ask pertinent questions about the strategy, how the team works (without being unduly personal) and how the company manages capital, revenue and, of course, therefore, cash. You should also do refresher field visits annually.

91: Audit committees

The audit and remuneration committees are two of the most important responsibilities of non-executive directors. I have chaired both, but today, if it is a public company, the chairman of the audit committee should be a qualified accountant. In both cases, you must never forget that you are there to look after the interests of shareholders.

A good audit committee's job is to be the board's eyes and ears on all financial matters. The committee must ensure a culture of no surprises for the main board, so that problems are identified and dealt with early. The committee should also be there to support and challenge the finance team, the internal audit department and the company's auditors.

Effective audit committees have never been more important than in this time of incredible turmoil in global financial markets. This should lead to a new era of focused financial attention and audit committees are set to become even more important and influential as part of strong effective boards. Managing uncertainty is a top priority for boards and audit committees.

RISK: THE NUMBER ONE PRIORITY

It is fundamental to ensure an appropriate understanding of the major risks facing the organisation, including lessons from global financial gyrations and corporate failings all around.

Does the company have good disaster recovery plans? Does the committee appreciate the company's risk culture beyond the boardroom? How does management ensure that "risk understanding" is articulated clearly throughout the company and embedded in the culture?

SIMPLE TIPS

As an audit committee member, you may be financially qualified, but do you spend enough time understanding the business and the people who run it? (With acknowledgement for some of the ideas below to KPMG, with whom I have had the pleasure of working.)

GET TO KNOW THE KEY PEOPLE

It is vital to develop strong relationships with the Chairman, the Chief Executive and the Finance Director – learn how they think, what motivates them and whether they are optimists, pessimists or realists. Try to understand their personal ambitions, which may reflect their actions. In addition, frequent informal communications with managers and auditors are very useful. Listen to what they say – or don't say. Read between the lines. You want to know about significant developments or information that is incorrect as early as possible.

UNDERSTAND THE BUSINESS PROPERLY

This is not just reading about the business, which of course is necessary, but finding time to visit different business units and also meet with customers, if possible.

EXERCISE SCEPTICISM

Don't just accept what people tell you. You want to find out what is behind the supposed facts and understand, from the information you gather, the company's risk profile. Scepticism is not being negative, but rather, it is a necessary challenge for directors to justify their financial models and projected outcomes. Very few financial outlines are conservative. Most people try to put the best company foot forward.

ACCOUNTABILITY

All directors need to realise that they are jointly and severally responsible for the welfare of the company and are accountable to the board. Ultimately, they are answerable to the shareholders and the board may not necessarily have similar goals to them. It is absolutely essential for the audit committee to be truly independent, with strong leadership at the helm.

RISK MANAGEMENT

To conclude, the audit committee is responsible for ensuring that intelligent risk management is in place. There needs to be a regular risk profile, which is proactively reviewed, updated and modified in line with changes to the business environment. Active risk management is the responsibility of all executives and will allow the company to have a strategic advantage over competitors. Last and very much not least, it is axiomatic that risk assessments will only be truly effective if they are undertaken by staff with the right mix of skills and, of course, supervised at board level by the appropriate people.

92: Remuneration committees

Remuneration is, of course, a highly emotive subject. Employees, very much including the chief executive and the executive board, want to earn as much as possible and will, at times, put a lot of psychological pressure on you. With the greed of recent years, we have seen excessive salaries, bonuses and long-term incentive payments.

It should be about finding a healthy balance between recruiting the right staff, paying them an attractive salary and motivating them to achieve, if not beat, the annual business plan and secure the long-term future of the company. They can be encouraged through the bonus and through the LTIP (Long-Term Incentive Plan), which usually allows them to build up shares in the company that they work for.

If the preoccupation of top management is with the bonus and the LTIP, then you clearly have the wrong people. A bonus is simply that – a bonus and not a right. Your job as head of the remuneration committee is to ensure the correct balance between now and the future, and while now is important for a company to grow and prosper, the future is what it is all about – not one year ahead, but three, five and beyond.

93: Private companies and financial responsibilities

When you join a board, you are jointly and severally responsible for the actions of the company. It is no longer about your department or direct responsibility. That is purely one part of the whole and you are by definition now involved in everything!

Many years ago, when Sir Anthony Tennant appointed me to the board of IDV (International Distillers & Vintners Ltd), he remarked, 'James, this is not a reward in itself, but the beginning of hard work and joint responsibility.' How right he was!

PRIVATE COMPANIES

If you are on the board of a private company, you may be asked by the bank to accept joint responsibility for any loan the bank advances the company. Be very wary before signing on the dotted line.

Once I had a very bad experience with a major bank when I was the nonexecutive Chairman of a start-up company in the educational field. We raised a bank loan of £100,000 and it was mutually agreed that as a 2.5% shareholder I would be limited to 2.5% of the risk.

Some years later, I resigned from the board because I did not like the way the company was being run and the family, who controlled the company, agreed that I would be absolved from responsibility. (I still have the letter.) Sadly, they never followed through properly and the banks can chase whoever they like.

Four years later, after the company failed, they chased me for £100,000 plus interest. I fortunately resolved the problem, but it was a very stressful time. You have been warned!

WINDING DOWN

I am glad I am not young... anymore.
Maurice Chevalier, actor

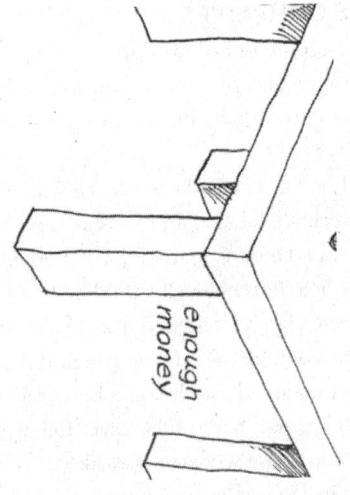

94: Making the break from corporate life

Far too many people struggle to make the transition to the "brave new normal" of family life. They find it very hard to live without the pros and cons of business.

Sometimes this is because they have been dismissed, or because retirement has arrived more quickly than anticipated and they had never given thought to or planned for it in any way. Whatever the reason, it can be a major shock to the system, from which some, sadly, never recover. I know because I got fired at fifty-five, and remained in deep shock for a while afterwards.

On the positive side, it made me realise who my friends and family are.

AMBITION IS A RAVENING BEAST THAT MUST BE KEPT IN CHECK

If you are upwardly mobile, egotistical and think you are wonderful, beware: pride comes before a fall. You may be Mr or Mrs Bigshot, with people bowing and scraping before you (a dangerous signal), but lose your job or move elsewhere and then you will find out who you can really depend upon.

You have only one life, so don't sacrifice it along with your family for the corporation. Of course, you want to be well paid and get the respect you deserve, but know you are dispensable and, ultimately, your family and friends are what counts.

They're the ones who will help and comfort you when you inevitably hit a road block or fall off track in your career. They're who will offer you support, wisdom and guidance, and they should always be your number-one priority.

So, always think carefully about your partner and children at home. Remember, you only borrow your children; eventually they will leave home, and if you have given them love, guidance and respect, they will repay it in kind. If you have purely regarded them as property and a necessary part of life, then you have got it entirely wrong.

THE RETURN OF THE FOUR-LEGGED TABLE

As you get older you might appreciate that a worthwhile and balanced life is like my friend the four-legged table:

Leg 1 – your family
Leg 2 – your friends
Leg 3 – your health
Leg 4 – enough money to enjoy the other three!

It is very sad if you have lots of money, but no family and poor health. Enjoy your time and keep things in perspective; there's no point in being the richest person in the cemetery!

95: It has to end sometime

Even if we don't formally retire, we all have to surrender to the inevitable at some point.

You may be the most important person in the company. You may have a regularly reserved table in a certain restaurant. You may be invited to all the important sports functions. You may puff yourself up and think how wonderful you are – but when you retire, you will be staggered by how few of those invitations come your way and how suddenly you are back to being Mr/Ms Nobody.

If you enjoy the journey and treat people with respect, you will receive your own reward as you pass through the University of Life.

96: Talent-spotting

As mentioned earlier, you should be nice to people as you climb the corporate ladder because, with a bit of luck, they may remember you on your way down. Having reached my seventies, I certainly find this appropriate.

I am now in chapter three of my life, or "the new direction".

We all have to start at the bottom (unless we are wrongly indulged by our parents). One of the great pleasures in my life is finding bright, young people with talent, treating them with respect and encouraging them to develop their full potential. Some of those people are in very senior positions today, and it is good to know that if I phone them and ask for help or advice, they are usually only too happy to see me.

I am no longer a senior executive in a major corporation, but it is rewarding to see the success of people who used to work with me many years ago in then-junior positions.

We are all social animals and if we treat all people with respect, it will make us more effective and happier as result.

97: There is no such thing as retirement, just a new direction

Experts say a happy retirement depends not on what you retire from, but what you retire to. It's a golden opportunity to stay fit and healthy and involve yourself in more meaningful work or activities, a second career or a lifelong dream.

PERSONAL HEALTH AND WELLBEING

Thanks to better lifestyles, food and medical care, people are living considerably longer than their forebears and, with luck on your side, you can plan to live beyond ninety. Of course, the genes we inherit are crucial, but we can do a lot to help ourselves by being both mentally and physically active. Barring medical reasons, everyone should take constructive exercise tailored to individual circumstances at least three times a week till the end of their days.

POST-RETIREMENT OR REDUNDANCY

You may be made redundant and/or forced to retire early. Take your time and smell the flowers – and also do some careful financial planning in order to enjoy the remaining chapters of your life.

Do a personal SWOT analysis (see Tip 2) and be ruthlessly honest to determine what you are good at during this stage of your life, and what you are not. This is no time for sentiment; rather, it's a time to face up to blunt reality.

THE NEW CAREER

On the work front, you should not allow yourself to come to a grinding halt. There is nothing worse than the bored, boring golfer who plays five times a week, and has little else to talk about.

Why not seek a new career? Depending on your experience you may be ideally placed to be a non-executive director. You may decide to put your time to good use and offer your services to an appropriate charity; you may choose to mentor young people, or you may even start your own small business – without risking all your hard-earned savings!

The real point is to do something active with your brain – you shouldn't go from hero to zero. I started my own business at the age of sixty-five, with a partner of a similar age and a third partner aged eighty-two. Yes, we had frustrations and issues to deal with and we were very much on our own without corporate support, but we had a lot of fun and, eight years later, sold the business to a dynamic international company, who continue to grow and build our brand.

A NEW BUSINESS?

You may have an exciting business idea. Do not hesitate to seek outside help and/or advice; you will probably need to talk to an accountant or a financial advisor. Remember, every new idea or company usually takes twice as long and twice as much money as you originally thought to break even. Many good business concepts fail simply because they run out of cash.

So, think carefully as you follow the new direction. Pure retirement is not an option for many people, unless you thrive on boredom or have great hobbies, which can be a career in themselves.

Whatever you decide to do, remember this good news: you no longer have to experience the daily commute, be involved in company politics or, in many cases, work with people you don't even like. This is an exciting opportunity, and what fun to be your own boss. So look at it positively and seize it. Carpe diem!

98: Self-employment v. corporate life

Assuming that you do want to be self-employed in one form or another, here are a few considerations, from my own experience:

- First and foremost, will you have an office at home or somewhere else? For obvious reasons, home is usually the cheapest option. Ideally, you need a separate room where you can hide yourself away with your computer, your books, your files and your thoughts. You may also want to start thinking about co-working spaces.
- If you were a very senior executive and had staff to look after you, it will be a rude awakening. Do not expect your partner to be your support/assistant, unless they wish to be and unless it is a commercial emergency.
- You are now self-employed, and mostly have to manage for yourself. There is no one to delegate to, and there is certainly no expense account. You cannot walk into the next-door office and chat to someone or meet at the office kitchen. I assume at the minimum you know how to switch on the kettle and make a cup of tea or coffee!
- We are very social by nature, and self-employment can be quite lonely. We do, however, at least have the telephone and the internet to keep in touch with people. So, brush up your IT and personal competences!
- If you start a business and are self-employed and wish to form a company, find a good, reliable accountant who will look after you without overcharging. I have been with the same small firm for twenty years and look forward to benefiting from their excellent support for many more years.
- While I do a lot of my own typing, I also have a part-time secretary who has her own workstation in a small office at my home. She looks after my books and does my major typing work and is generally a friend and a support. I pay her by the hour and it is a mutually-beneficial arrangement.
- If you want to travel anywhere, plan it and make the necessary arrangements yourself. I schedule my own trips, but also use a small travel agency who support me, when required. For domestic travel, I use my own car or public transport, but if I do need someone to take me to the airport, I have a personal arrangement with a small chauffeur service. All expenses are, of course, for your own account, so with a good accountant and careful management you'll soon

learn what is legally a tax-deductible expense or not, and this can be a very important consideration as you grow your tiny business.

At least, for better or for worse, I am answerable to myself, hardly ever have to wear a suit, and have a short walk to the office!

99: You never stop learning

Learning doesn't stop when you have had enough. That is when it truly begins.

In today's world of exponential speed and dynamism, existing knowledge is soon out of date. You have to constantly refresh yourself.

You may learn as a hobby – like a foreign language, which should give you satisfaction and enhance your travel experiences – or you may pick up a skill which will make life rewarding, be it in the IT field, or perhaps something as domestic as improving your gardening knowledge or cooking skills.

Depending on where you are, if you contact the local authorities and also search the net, you will find opportunities for self-improvement, many of which incur minimal (if any) cost.

So many people think they know it all, which should prompt a serious red warning light. We must remain constantly curious and interested in others. I still know very little and need to keep learning.

Even if you are fully retired, you can learn a great deal through younger friends and your children, which will, in turn, make life more interesting and rewarding.

There is no time like the present – start now!

100: Anno Domini: Father Time and the art of the possible

While it is good to be an optimist, as life moves on and as we get older, we should all be more aware of the art of the possible, rather than what is ideal. Push the boundaries and chase your dreams, but remember they are tempered, whether you like it or not, by your age, your circumstances and your health. Do what you can to keep active and enjoy the journey.

HOW TO LIVE WITH YOUR PARTNER AFTER RETIREMENT

The old clichés are still relevant today: "I married you for love, but not for lunch", and "I love you every day but not all day!"

Partners of the recently retired, who are used to having the run of the house all day, suddenly find there is another person they're stumbling over – a person who, for example, rushes out of sheer curiosity to be first to answer the phone (because morning phone calls have always been for them for the past thirty years). Being sensitive about this and many other aspects of the new life is crucial for domestic balance and harmony.

LAST WILL AND TESTAMENT

Finally, make sure your will is up to date, or even that you have one. The number of retirees I meet who have not even drawn up a will is incredible. It is thoughtless and selfish and creates problems for those left behind.

CONCLUSION

We play for the pleasure of winning and for the gratification of playing.
Peter Fleck, Director of The Last Drop Distillers

The above quote, from my good friend of more than fifty years, is most appropriate. Hopefully, we all have long and positive careers which are financially and emotionally rewarding. At the end of the day, your career and your marriage/family are probably the two most important and enduring aspects of your life.

I trust this book has given you some clues and tips to help you get more out of your career and your journey through life. I would also hope that it will be a useful reference for you as you deal with many of the issues and opportunities mentioned herein.

Final thoughts

In this complex world we would all like to find the "magic bullet", the quick and simple formula for success. There is no such thing, or life would be far too easy – and far too boring.

If this book has been of use, I hope it is in appreciating that virtually everything in business is about brands and people, and great leaders motivate people to do extraordinary things in order to satisfy the people that really matter: the consumers. Further, brands have to be kept in a state of constant repair. This applies to "brand you" as much as it does to any product.

In the various businesses in which you operate, the generation of sustainable cash will be the true measure of success. Without cash, one simply cannot survive.

As you climb the leadership ladder, never forget from whence you come and the importance of building strong teams and sharing the glory. We all have egos, but it is important for them to be kept in control. You must behave as you wish to become.

Adhere to sound business principles and ensure that your plans are well executed to improve the odds of success. Little sound steps on the journey are crucial, and you must keep learning, be courageous and make the necessary changes in yourself to be a winner.

Good luck as you make your mark on your journey. May it all be challenging, interesting, rewarding and fun. May you make a positive contribution to society and for many, many years have a fulfilled and balanced career and a long and happy life.

ACKNOWLEDGEMENTS

I have read countless books and articles during my fifty years in business, and have, over time, picked up comments which resonate with my experience. Most of my observations and thoughts, however, have come from my travels, work experience and the pleasure of working with diverse cultures and people around the globe. At no time has there been a deliberate attempt to adopt the work of others.

This book could not have come to fruition without the help of others. A number of my friends have graciously read early drafts and given me their blunt opinions. In particular, I would like to mention Arthur Shapiro, Ben Howkins, Alistair Delves and Cara Bradley.

I would also like to mention Katie Taylor, who spent many hours updating and editing this book. A big thank you.

And last but not least, my secretary and friend Christine Holland, who has put up with my mutterings for twenty years, and my wife Celia and our daughters Caroline and Jessica, for their patience…

1.24